		Date Due	JUL 2000
		JUN	2004
		JUNI X X 2015	

TWENTIETH CENTURY INTERPRETATIONS
OF

THE
AMBASSADORS

A Collection of Critical Essays

Edited by
ALBERT E. STONE, JR.

Prentice-Hall, Inc. *Englewood Cliffs, N. J.*

A SPECTRUM BOOK

Copyright © 1969 by Prentice-Hall, Inc., Englewood Cliffs, New Jersey. A
SPECTRUM BOOK. All rights reserved. No part of this book may be reproduced
in any form or by any means without permission in writing from the publisher.
P 13-023929-1; C 13-023937-2. *Library of Congress Catalog Card Number 69-15349.*
Printed in the United States of America.

Current printing (last number):

10 9 8 7 6 5 4 3 2 1

Prentice-Hall International, Inc. (*London*)

Contents

Introduction, *by Albert E. Stone, Jr.*

PART ONE—*View Points*

PART TWO—*Interpretations*

Introduction

by *Albert E. Stone, Jr.*

Henry James considered *The Ambassadors* his most successful novel
—"frankly, quite the best, 'all round,' of my productions," he wrote
in the Preface to the New York Edition. This judgment, coming from
a novelist who was also a distinguished literary critic, has naturally
carried much weight with readers. Yet from the beginning—in fact,
even before the publication of *The Ambassadors* in 1903—the book
attracted opponents nearly as determined as its defenders.

Henry M. Alden began the controversy in 1900 with his famous
memorandum for Harper and Brothers, to whom James had submitted
an elaborate 20,000-word "Project" or scenario for the novel he
hoped would appear serially in *Harper's Magazine*. Alden advised
his fellow editors against acceptance. "The tissues of it are too subtly
fine for general appreciation. It is subjective, fold within fold of a
complex mental web, in which the reader is lost if his much-wearied
attention falters. . . . We ought to do better." Nearly fifty years
later, F. O. Matthiessen and Kenneth B. Murdock attacked Alden's
report as "a masterpiece of miscomprehension." "All the stock preju-
dices against James' international material are there," they declared,
"and no indication that Strether, whose central consciousness marks
James' final perfection of his method, even figures in the novel." [1]
These opposing views of James's achievement in *The Ambassadors*
are typical. They mark the limits of critical controversy which has
continued for nearly seventy years, producing the most extensive
and varied chapter in the whole book of Jamesian criticism. The
essays and comments in this collection comprise some, but by no
means all, of the highpoints of this controversy.[2]

[1] See *The Notebooks of Henry James*, eds. F. O. Matthiessen and Kenneth B.
Murdock (New York, 1947), p. 372.
[2] For a reasonably complete bibliography of material on *The Ambassadors* see
the following: *Articles on American Literature*, ed. Lewis Leary (Durham, N.C.,
1954), pp. 155–65; Eunice C. Hamilton, "Biographical and Critical Studies of Henry
James, 1941–1948," *American Literature*, XX (January, 1949), 424–35; Viola R. Dun-
bar, "Addenda to 'Biographical and Critical Studies of Henry James, 1941–1948,'"

Alden's advice was heeded and *The Ambassadors,* instead of making
its debut in *Harper's,* came out finally in the *North American Review,*
an eminently respectable but much less popular journal to which
James's long-time friend, William Dean Howells, was literary consul-
tant and contributor. It ran, somewhat abbreviated in length, for
twelve issues—January through December, 1903. This initial appearance was significant in at least two ways. First, it foretold the novel's
future audience. From the beginning, *The Ambassadors* has appealed
to a smaller, more select audience than most masterpieces of American
fiction. In 1903, the initial critical response—especially in the genteel
journals—was enthusiastic, but no reviewer was under the illusion
that James's new novel would appeal to a wide audience.[3] Over the
years the situation has not radically altered. *The Ambassadors* is
admired but widely unread. Today, in spite of half a dozen paperback
editions, *The Ambassadors* remains very much a *succès d'estime,* less
popular, even in the universities, than *The Portrait of a Lady.* The
Harpers knew their American audience when they decided on the
North American Review as the right magazine for *The Ambassadors.*

Ironically, the man who arranged for *The Ambassadors* to appear
in the *North American Review* was himself the remote, unwitting
source for the story. As James records in his notebooks, Howells
originally uttered Strether's famous outcry. "Oh, you are young, you
are young—be glad of it: be glad of it and *live,*" the aging novelist
was reported to have said to Jonathan Sturges as they sat in a
Parisian garden in 1894. This simple piece of advice, couched, as
many of James's key statements are, in the form of a cliché, becomes
the announced theme or issue of James's story. Lambert Strether, of
course, is differentiated in many ways from the American editor whose
sentiment he echoes. James made this clear in a letter to Howells in
August, 1901, in which he specified that his friend's remark had
become "the mere point of the *start,* of a subject."[4] In spite of this

---

American Literature, XXII (March, 1950), 56–61; *Modern Fiction Studies,* III
(Spring, 1957), 81–82; *Modern Fiction Studies,* XII (Spring, 1966), 136–38; and current bibliographies in *American Literature* and *PMLA.*

[3] See Richard N. Foley, *Criticism in American Periodicals of the Works of Henry
James from 1866 to 1916* (Washington, D.C., 1944), pp. 92–97.

Doubleday explained this lack of popular appeal: few persons under thirty
would enjoy it because they could not understand it; and of those above thirty
only those who had in some way surrendered to the spell of Europe and those
who had a high degree of culture could appreciate it. The *Literary World* further limited the prospective readers: no patriotic American could stand it; few
women would like it; no business man could find time to read it; and no one
lacking a sense of humor could follow it. [pp. 92–93, footnote]

[4] *The Letters of Henry James,* ed. Percy Lubbock (New York, 1920), I, 376.

disclaimer, however, several echoes reverberate between the "*désorienté elderly American*" of this novel and the distinguished editor-novelist. For one thing, the review Strether edits in Woollett seems to be a country cousin to the *North American Review*. For another, the mixed tone of amused sympathy and detached irony which James takes toward Strether is very close to the tone he privately took toward Howells. James had a lifelong respect for his friend, but his sense of Howells' limitations was even stronger. The most amusing side of Howells' provincialism to James was his prudery. When it came to deciding how to involve an imaginative provincial like Strether in Parisian life, James must have recalled Howells' particular squeamishness about European sexual customs. Although himself a terrible prude, James enjoyed observing his friend's far greater naïveté and reticence. Once he noted with amusement Howells' horrified reaction to an Edmond de Goncourt novel which has a scene laid in a "whorehouse *de province*." On another occasion James took malicious delight in relaying to Howells the inquiry of a French baroness who wished to know if incest was a good theme for a novel.[5] James takes a similar secret pleasure in Strether's refined blindness to the realities of Chad's liaison. Like Howells, Strether wants "life" but finds himself unprepared for the form in which it actually comes.

Though the figure of Howells lurks more palpably in the shadows of Gloriani's garden than some readers realize, the stronger parallel between character and prototype involves, of course, James himself. In fact, Strether shares so many qualities and beliefs with his creator that there is still wide acceptance of Joseph Warren Beach's early assertion: "If there is one of his characters whom we are tempted to identify with James himself, it is Lambert Strether." [6] James, moreover, encouraged the identification. Writing to a friend about *The Ambassadors*, he closed by referring to the "poor old hero, in whom you will perhaps find a vague resemblance (though not facial!) to your always/Henry James." [7] Anyone familiar with even the main features of the novelist's life knows that the resemblances, though never exact, are more than vague. They flow from the essential fact that Strether reenacts James's own discovery of the limits of all human societies and the higher claims of the individual imagination. That is to say, both possess, in spite of all qualifications, romantic temperaments.

[5] See Leon Edel, *Henry James: The Conquest of London: 1870–1881* (Philadelphia, 1962), pp. 216–17; also *The Untried Years*, p. 274.

[6] J. W. Beach, *The Method of Henry James* (New Haven, 1918), p. 269.

[7] HJ to Jocelyn Persse, in *Selected Letters of Henry James*, ed. Leon Edel (Garden City, N.Y., 1960), p. 193.

Strether makes this discovery in the innocent spirit of a young man who, in point of fact, is fifty-five years old. In creating such an unusual protagonist, James drew on a wide range of personal experience from earliest childhood to his most recent past. Though born in New York City in 1843, James insisted that his first childhood memory was of the Place Vendôme. He had been taken there as a baby by his eccentric father, Henry James Sr., in line with that systematically unsystematic way of life which made him a citizen of the James family but not really of any class or nation. After this prophetic glimpse of Europe, James spent most of his childhood in his native city, in the district around Washington Square, but between twelve and seventeen he lived abroad—in London, Paris, Windsor, Boulogne, Bonn, Geneva. Henry's formal education, on both sides of the Atlantic, consisted of a bewildering succession of governesses, tutors, and schools, for no institution or individual could match the utopian requirements of his father. Shortly before the Civil War, the James family returned to America and settled finally in Cambridge. There the future novelist established, briefly, an institutional tie: he attended for one year the Harvard Law School. He never joined a church or a political party, and an injury to his back made army service out of the question. Such a life style gave James a unique sense of freedom—and isolation— from all those groups and allegiances which together form the "tin mould" into which Strether feels one's consciousness to be poured. Freedom to live independently of both Woollett and Paris, of both America *and* Europe, was something James learned early, so that by 1878 he was able to write, somewhat smugly as Christof Wegelin points out, "There comes a time when one set of customs, wherever it may be found, grows to seem about as provincial as another." [8]

Learning the pleasures and the cost of the imaginative, transnational life threw James—as it throws Strether—necessarily into the role of an observer who lives chiefly by "seeing" into experience from the outside. The price of this was considerable. It involved renouncing marriage, a settled way of life, and other modes of possession. This sense of pleasures foregone and ties denied was strong in James, and the writer's own divided emotions lend force to his protagonist's final scene with Maria Gostrey. For, after thirty years of a peripatetic life, James, only four years before beginning *The Ambassadors,* had settled down at Lamb House, Rye, in Sussex, to taste at least some of the joys Strether denies himself in Maria's snug apartment.

Living intensely through the eye of the mind offers only a certain kind of freedom, as both James and Strether recognize. The elderly

[8] C. Wegelin, *The Image of Europe in Henry James* (Dallas, 1958), p. 87.

American's plea to Little Bilham contains, as some critics forget, both the injunction to live and frank recognition of the tin mould, Strether's figure for limiting circumstance. James himself once used another figure. "I regard the march of history," he once wrote Charles Eliot Norton, "very much as a man placed astride of a locomotive, without knowledge or help, would regard the progress of that vehicle. To stick on, somehow, and even enjoy the scenery as we pass, is the sum of my aspiration." [9] As Leon Edel has written, this early statement of James's reflects the "vision of a comparatively happy observer and artist" who has selected the life of active contemplation, fatalistically aware that his freedom to do so is illusory. Something of that blend of fatalism and freedom—found also in William James's pragmatism—is acquired by Lambert Strether. Indeed, one way to define the fictional experience through which James leads his hero is to call it "the making at an advanced age of a pragmatist."

For imaginative pragmatists like James and Strether, *where* experience occurs is nearly as important as the shape of experience itself. For both, Paris is so central a feature of awakening that many readers will agree with Beach's remark that "the subject of this study is Paris. It is Paris that gives its particular tone and color to this work." [10] Place and process are almost one in *The Ambassadors*. This fact reflects the author's personal experience as well as his acceptance of the folk tales about what happens to Americans in Paris. One of James's oldest and most vivid recollections of Paris dated from the winter of 1857, when the James family lived there. Sometime during that season the thirteen-year-old boy, already a confirmed spectator, took a long walk with his brother William along the Left Bank, down the Rue de Tournon, past the Café Foyot to the Luxembourg Palace. Strether duplicates that walk in the second book of *The Ambassadors*. James's luminous, detailed evocation of the Parisian scene as Strether first encounters it combines the remembered freshness of a boy's vision with the energy of adult nostalgia and discrimination.

Other more recent Parisian memories provided James with the setting and several characters for the central scene of *The Ambassadors*. In 1876, James had gone to tea at Madame Mohl's salon in the Rue du Bac. From her windows he remembered looking down into a garden where young novitiates from a nearby seminary strolled beneath old trees. Some years later, James walked that same lawn when, in the spring of 1893, he visited Whistler's "queer little garden-house" in the Rue du Bac. From the painter's garden James looked up at

---

[9] Quoted in Leon Edel, *The Conquest of London*, pp. 165–66.
[10] *The Method of Henry James*, p. 267.

the window from which he had once looked down. His memory of aristocratic ladies, of artists, and of an ancient garden fused with the other elements of the imagined scene to form the rich moment of Strether's awakening which takes place in Gloriani's garden.

These links between author and character give a special personal dimension to the action of this novel, which the writer's imagination had summoned up in other variations many times before 1900. In a sense, James had spent thirty years preparing to write *The Ambassadors*. As early as 1874, in "Madame de Mauves," he had created in Longmore an innocent adult American whose involvement in the foreign marriage of Euphemia de Mauves ends in renunciation and withdrawal. The opposite impulse—toward commitment—is comically expressed in "A Bundle of Letters" (1879), in which Louis Leverett writes what is essentially a parody of Strether's declaration to Little Bilham. In longer narratives of this period, too, James dramatized related themes of Europe and the imaginative life, marriage as commitment and renunciation. *Roderick Hudson* (1875), *The American* (1877), *The Portrait of a Lady* (1881) all anticipate some of the central features of *The Ambassadors*. During the eighties and nineties, James's career took other turns, but in *The Sacred Fount,* written just before *The Ambassadors,* he experimented—unsuccessfully, as many readers feel—with a narrative rigidly restricted in point of view and with an action curiously like that of its successor. The forward trajectory of James's imagination is seen in "The Beast in the Jungle," written the year *The Ambassadors* was completed. Here John Marcher's pathetic realization of a wasted life of noninvolvement and May Bartram's sacrificial spectatorship are tragic reprises of the relationship between Strether and Maria Gostrey.

The progression from "Madame de Mauves" through *The Ambassadors* to "The Beast in the Jungle" marks but one pattern in James's fiction. More important, however, than such parallels and prefigurations are the decided differences between virtually all James's early work and *The Ambassadors*. These include the stylistic developments and embellishments lumped under the term "James's later period," as well as the psychological nuances of character treatment that accompany and explain that style. Austin Warren has succinctly identified the circumstances in the author's life that help to account for these new literary characteristics: the gradual loss of a popular audience, the author's satiety with English social life and his settling at Rye, the disastrous attempts to write for the London theater, the shift from writing to dictation as a compositional method, inspiration from younger writers (like Stevenson, Conrad, Ford, and Crane) embued with the new symbolist aesthetics, and more remote but still

palpable influences of Maeterlinck, Ibsen, and Nathaniel Hawthorne.[11]
Identifying these forces and events in the nineties by no means
accounts for the new ground James broke with *The Ambassadors*.
Though in social behavior and philosophy a passive rather than an
aggressive mind, James's artistic imagination was experimental, active, innovative—and never more so than during the composition of
this novel. The fullness of the record of his creative process during
these few years attests to the vitality of his imagination as it progressively recognized, defined, related, and finally expressed the elements
of Strether's situation in the final form of *The Ambassadors*. Critics
disagree about the worth of that final form. But those acquainted
with James's whole creative experience as successively revealed in the
notebooks, the "Project" sent to *Harper's*, the serial and first edition
versions of the novel, in the Preface to the later New York Edition,
and in letters to friends, agree that "James knew exactly what he
wished to do, and did it with extraordinary perfection." [12]
The record begins with the germ James recorded in his notebooks
on October 31, 1895. Here we see an author seizing and defining the
emotional center of a story in remarkably complete terms. His protagonist's age, temperament, occupation, and past are all quickly
specified and related to the "little situation" in the garden. James sees
the banality of Paris as the setting but, after considering alternates,
tells himself "I'm afraid it *must* be Paris; if he's an American." The
principal changes between this outline and the completed story are,
first, the relatively scant attention James ultimately pays to Strether's
"*other* relation"—his private past of family failures and sacrifices,
and second, the much expanded story of his "dumb passion of desire,
of I don't know what." There is, in short, less Woollett and more Paris
in the final version. Madame de Vionnet is conspicuously absent from
the germ of *The Ambassadors,* but clearly there from the start is the
mixed ironic tone James intends to maintain toward his protagonist.
This makes understandable, therefore, the author's final, firm intention to have his hero sacrifice himself and his hopes for mere happiness. "It is too late, too late *now,* for HIM to live." Strether's last
meeting with Maria Gostrey, which was later to distress critics as
diverse as Yvor Winters, F. O. Matthiessen, and F. R. Leavis, is determined from the outset. From this conviction James never wavered.
The "Project of a Novel by Henry James," sent to *Harper's* in
September, 1900, is a unique document which should be consulted by
all serious readers of *The Ambassadors*. For perhaps no other work

---

[11] Austin Warren, "Symbolic Imagery," in Leon Edel, ed., *Henry James: A Collection of Critical Essays* (Englewood Cliffs, N.J., 1963), p. 123.
[12] Orlo Williams, *"The Ambassadors," The Criterion*, VIII (September, 1928), 54.

in American literature is there a comparably complete working plan
or scenario. It indicates one benefit James derived from his unhappy
flirtation with the stage. (Running to some ninety pages in the
original typescript, the "Project" is too long for inclusion here, but
can be found in *The Notebooks of Henry James.*) Since it was written
to plead the novel's case for serial publication, the "Project" is an important critical statement as well as a guide to James's creative process.
As Edna Kenton points out, "with James the process of criticism—
which is nothing, ever, but appreciation of the thing criticised—not
only preceded but was an inherent part of creation itself." [13]

Serialization offered and required symmetry of form. James sees
his story organized into ten equal parts (or perhaps twelve), each
consisting of two chapters. This would mean a narrative of 100,000
or 120,000 words. The finished work is not quite so shapely as the
"Project" proposes; it grew longer, as was usually the case with James,
and some of the twelve books came to contain as many as five chapters.
But the main goal was achieved: the action is arranged into twelve
more or less equal scenes, "each very full, as it were, and charged—
like a rounded medallion, in a series of a dozen, hung, with its effect
of high relief, on a wall." Matthiessen's discussion of this achieved
"roundness of structure" shows how ingeniously the novelist met the
challenge of monthly installments with the required pattern of regu-
larly spaced complications and climaxes. Another positive virtue of
serial publication in James's eyes was that it permitted ample space
and time in which the story might unfold. "I find that the very most
difficult thing in the art of the novelist," he later wrote the Duchess
of Sutherland, "is to give the impression and illusion of the real
lapse of time." The novel's leisurely pace results, then, not simply
from James's elaborate style or from the nature of his theme but
also from the magazine format in which it was originally framed.

A second important argument the "Project" makes is a case for the
proposed novel's popular appeal. Here James amplifies previously
unexplored relations of Strether to the women in his life. Much
subsequent discussion of *The Ambassadors* has turned on these relationships. Two issues have engrossed attention: the degree to which
Strether is thought to have fallen in love (perhaps unconsciously)
with Marie de Vionnet, and, second, the gratuitous cruelty or at least
the inappropriateness of his rejection of Maria Gostrey in the final
scene of the book. On both matters James's prior intent, if not his
accomplished action, is clear. Madame de Vionnet, he writes,

[13] Edna Kenton, *"The Ambassadors:* Project of Novel," *Hound and Horn,* VII
(April–June, 1934), 542.

strikes our hero from the first—which is the most particular note of all
—as a kind of person he has absolutely never seen, nor ever, with any
distinctness, dreamed of. And yet it's not in the least that he has fallen
in love with her, or is at all likely to do so. Her charm is independent of
that for him and gratifies some more distinctively disinterested aesthetic,
intellectual, social, even, so to speak, historic sense in him, which has
never yet been, *à pareille fête,* never found itself so called to the front.[14]

That James forgot or betrayed this promise is the assumption of
several critics. With respect to Maria Gostrey, too, James paints in
the proposed picture "with a single touch of the brush." His hero
cannot marry "poor convenient, amusing, unforgettable, impossible
Gostrey." James will show Strether's moment of hesitation but cannot
concede more to popular romance.

> He *can't* accept or assent. He won't. He doesn't. It's too late. It mightn't
> have been, sooner—but it is, yes, distinctly, now. He has come so far
> through his total little experience that he has come out on the other
> side—on the other side, even, of a union with Miss Gostrey.[15]

The "Project" concludes on this note. *The Ambassadors* is to be a
"drama of discriminations," not one of ordinary Parisian passions.
James will not go very far in meeting the expectations of readers of
sentimental romances like George Du Maurier's *Trilby.*

With a scenario in hand of the length and fullness of his "Project"
and with a theme and central character congenial to his imagination,
James proceeded with remarkable ease and speed to the actual composition of *The Ambassadors.* The writing was apparently accomplished between September, 1900, and June or July, 1901. Later, in
the Preface to the New York Edition, James recalled his sense of
"absolute conviction" and "constant clearness" which prevailed during
these months, "like a monotony of fine weather." "Nothing resisted,
nothing betrayed," he exulted; "it shed from any side I could turn
it to the same golden glow." All the biographical evidence we have
suggests that *The Ambassadors* caused its creator none of the difficulties
and delays which beset Herman Melville in the writing of *Moby-Dick*
or Mark Twain in the even more protracted writing of *Adventures
of Huckleberry Finn.* That James recalled the composition so pleasantly tells us, of course, nothing of literary value about the book. Yet
knowledge of the author's feelings may well have encouraged critics
like F. W. Dupee in the conviction that *"The Ambassadors* is mainly

---

[14] *Notebooks,* p. 392.
[15] *Notebooks,* pp. 414–15.

comedy . . . and its attractions are the appropriate ones of grace and clarity." [16]

But the next critical stage in the growth of the novel—that of its publication in 1903—introduces serious questions about the "clarity" if not the "grace" of James's story. Publication came in three forms, all distinct from each other. First was the serial version in the *North American Review,* followed by the English edition in September and then by the first American edition in November. From a critical perspective, the serial version is interesting because more than three of the thirty-six chapters were omitted in order to fit the magazine's limitations of space. As S. P. Rosenbaum has observed, the omitted portions of the novel indicate what the author considered "if not unimportant, at least somehow separate and detachable." [17] These omitted chapters, all set in Paris, largely concern Strether's growing relations with Chad Newsome. Consequently, the novel's first readers received a clearer, fuller picture of Lambert Strether's involvement with Marie de Vionnet and Maria Gostrey than with the charming Chad. Years later, in the letter to Hugh Walpole reprinted here, James admits that "the relation of Chad to Strether is a limited and according to my method only implied and indicated thing." Readers, too, have followed James in paying much more attention to Strether's other connections than to this particular one.

A far more significant difference, however, between the three 1903 versions of *The Ambassadors* is the fact that the first American edition contains a misplaced chapter. Chapter XXVIII, one of those kept out of the magazine, was replaced *after* Chapter XXIX. Furthermore, this Harper edition, rather than the English Methuen edition in which the mistake was not made, formed the basic text for James's revisions in the New York Edition of 1907–1909—where the same mistake occurs again. The error escaped everyone, apparently, including Henry James himself, until 1950, when it was detected by Robert E. Young, a Stanford undergraduate. Leon Edel summarizes in "The Text of *The Ambassadors*" the circumstances leading to this lapse, the responsibility for which he properly lays at the door of Harper's. Nevertheless some important questions remain. How much "clarity" of style or plot does *The Ambassadors* actually exhibit if two generations of readers can fail to note the misplacement or reversal of two chapters? Does not this support Alden's original criticism? How careful were James's proofreadings and revisions if his acknowledged favorite

[16] F. W. Dupee, *Henry James, His Life and Writings* (Garden City, N.Y., 1956), p. 214.

[17] "Textual Commentary," in *The Ambassadors* (Norton Critical Edition; New York, 1964), p. 356.

went through both processes with this flaw uncorrected? How closely, in fact, has the text of *The Ambassadors* been read by its various admirers and detractors? Without exaggerating the magnitude of the original error, one can indeed recognize the force of these queries. Leon Edel concludes with justice: "one would think that our scholars and critics would determine first what their text is, before they start their explications."

If critics and scholars have ignored the texts of *The Ambassadors*, they cannot be accused of ignoring the Preface James wrote to his New York Edition of the novel. Indeed, this essay has probably defined and directed discussion of *The Ambassadors* more than any other written analysis. James approaches his own work without any preconceived pattern or critical dogma. Rather he discusses the finished story as the expression of a particular set of problems. The only theory at work seems to be that stated in the concluding sentence: "the Novel remains still, under the right persuasion, the most independent, most elastic, most prodigious of literary forms." James describes how he pragmatically constructed his tale, building forward and backward from the scene in the garden. Thus the author's creative and critical practice are precisely the same open, experimental one which Strether learns to adopt in the course of the action. In this sense, *The Ambassadors* is both the least and most philosophical of novels.

James identifies the "major propriety" of his story as the decision to employ but one center of consciousness and to keep "it all within my hero's compass." Dilating upon the "splendid particular economy" of this arrangement, James differentiates it from mere first-person narrative or omniscient third-person narrative. Neither is James's method to be confused with what would soon after come to be called "stream of consciousness." Instead of the "terrible *fluidity* of self-revelation" which would result from making Strether fully and completely "hero and historian," James decided to establish a perspective outside of the protagonist's consciousness but focused upon that consciousness "from beginning to end without intermission or deviation," so that "every grain" of it might be directly expressed. By "every grain," however, James means only conscious thought and imagination, not subconscious feelings or urges. *The Ambassadors* is the map of a mind, not of a psyche. This fictional point of view, its precise nature and function, its success or failure, has been a crucial issue in critical controversy. For one group, including Joseph Warren Beach, Percy Lubbock, and Richard P. Blackmur, James accomplished brilliantly the feat of maintaining focus upon one mind. In doing so he helped to create the characteristic method of the modern novel as practiced later by Joyce, Gide, Kafka, Faulkner, and others. Percy Lubbock, in

The Craft of Fiction, makes the classic *apologia* for point of view in
The Ambassadors. It is a story, he concludes,

> which is seen from one man's point of view, and yet a story in which
> that point of view is itself a matter for the reader to confront and to
> watch constructively. Everything in the novel is now dramatically ren-
> dered, whether it is a page of dialogue or a page of description, because
> even in the page of description nobody is addressing us, nobody is re-
> porting his impression to the reader. The impression is enacting itself
> in the endless series of images that play over the outspread expanse of
> the man's mind and memory. . . . And yet *as a whole* the book is all
> pictorial, an indirect impression received through Strether's intervening
> consciousness, beyond which the story never strays.[18]

A very different critique is advanced in John E. Tilford's essay
reprinted in this collection. Unlike many readers before him who
appear to have taken James—and Lubbock—at their word, Tilford
measures the Preface of *The Ambassadors* carefully against the text.
He proves conclusively that James assumed more rigor in point of
view than he actually practiced. Joan Bennett, among others, had
earlier noted exceptions to James's asserted consistency, but Tilford
makes the most complete examination of James's lapses. He concludes
that, far from being an impersonal artist like Joyce, James remained,
in *The Ambassadors* at least, remarkably Victorian in technique, at
times "almost as affably omniscient as Thackeray." Authorial interven-
tions, remarks to the reader, and shifts away from Strether's point of
view are more frequent in *The Ambassadors* than either author or
the average reader has recognized.

The Strether-centered point of view James adopted and, in spite
of lapses, largely adhered to, dictated several other literary arrangements. One of the most obvious is the usual Jamesian confidante. *The
Ambassadors* has two—Waymarsh, one of the simplest characters in
the novel, and Maria Gostrey, one of the more complex. Like the
"Project," the confidante or *ficelle* here (and in other late works) is
partly a legacy from James's theatrical writing, but partly also a development out of the earlier fiction. Given an indirect, dramatic
narrative, the reader's need for a character who can draw out the
hero is obvious. But the case of Maria Gostrey is almost unique in
the degree to which a serviceable minor figure flowered in the course
of the story, assuming by the end "something of the dignity of a
prime idea." James confesses to a "deep dissimulation" in making Miss
Gostrey's role thus organic to the story. Recognizing that the final
scene is crucial for the success of this deception, James invites the

---

[18] *The Craft of Fiction* (New York, 1921), p. 171.

reader to share the "fun" and "interest" of "such at once 'creative' and critical questions as how and where and why to make Miss Gostrey's false connexion carry itself, under a due high polish, as a real one." Many readers find the falsity of Maria's formal function less disturbing than the false morality—as they see it—which this relationship produces at the denouement. Strether's rejection of Maria's offer of love and security strikes many, including sympathetic readers like Matthiessen, as artificial, gratuitous, even morally outrageous. Frequently such a judgment rests upon appreciating Maria as "a norm of moral evaluation," to quote Sister M. Corona Sharp, or as the bridge between the worlds of Paris and Woollett, as U. C. Knoepflmacher believes.[19] Taking such a view of Miss Gostrey usually means being less sympathetic both to Strether and to Marie de Vionnet.

A natural result of confining the narration to Strether's perspective and then equipping him with conversational confederates is a plot in which scenes of direct action alternate with discussion or description. Or, as James himself explains, "everything in it that is not scene (not, I of course mean, complete and functional scene, treating *all* the submitted matter, as by logical start, logical turn, and logical finish) is discriminated preparation, is the fusion and synthesis of picture. These alternations propose themselves all recognizably, I think, from an early stage, as the very form and figure of *The Ambassadors.*" James's sense of symmetry which also fits neatly the requirements of serial publication, influenced the plot in other respects. These have been analyzed by many critics, most notably by Percy Lubbock and E. M. Forster. Forster's description of the plot of *The Ambassadors* as resembling an hourglass, with Paris at the center and Strether and Chad moving gracefully, like dancers, into each other's position, is well known, though many readers of *Aspects of the Novel* may not agree with Forster's assessment of the price paid for such symmetry. Matthiessen and Dupee are more sympathetic critics who find the plot of this novel perfectly designed and proportioned. E. K. Brown's description, included here, of James's use of gradation and surprise in his manipulation of plot and character is still another answer to the strictures of Forster, though based on the same sense of Jamesian pattern. Maxwell Geismar, on the other hand, is least impressed of all the critics with the "architectural roundness" of *The Ambassadors.* In his eyes, the celebrated method of alternation is simply James's disguise for a story in which "content has ebbed away. . . . It is quite possible to omit several rings of the exposition without doing much harm to the story's meaning." Certainly James would have been

---

[19] See Sister M. Corona Sharp, *The Confidante in Henry James: Evolution and Moral Value of a Fictive Character* (Notre Dame, 1963), p. 177.

dismayed to hear that *any* of the scenes between his hero and Maria Gostrey could be called mere "skippable exposition."

Though the Preface discusses point of view and narrative form as these relate to the three principal characters, James also tries to demonstrate the organic connections of lesser characters to the action. Here he is anxious to point out the importance of Mrs. Newsome to the achieved form of his novel. The title itself suggests her role as the source of money and morality for the world of Woollett. But James confesses concern that readers clearly perceive the exquisite appropriateness for this story of a major figure who never appears. Her part, he pleads, is essential to the composition—and "composition alone is positive beauty." In this light, he sees her as a technical triumph, her very absence "no less intensely than circuitously present through the whole thing." Mrs. Newsome thus highlights two other "mysteries" in the story—the actual nature of the relationship Strether observes between her son and the French Countess, and the unnamed article of manufacture on which her fortune is based. Many critics accept the author's assessment of Mrs. Newsome as an effective dramatic device. Oscar Cargill, in *The Novels of Henry James,* shows persuasively James's debt here to Ibsen, particularly to *Rosmersholm,* for the prototype of an absent, mysterious moral force.[20]

Another lesser figure whose place in the completed picture bothers James is Chad Newsome. Though less concerned in this case with the possible reactions of readers, like S. Gorley Putt, who think *The Ambassadors* ought to have been Chad's story not Strether's, James does nevertheless acknowledge his partial failure to show Chad to *"proportional* advantage." [21] We have already noted James's willingness to sacrifice Chad in the chapters selected to be dropped from the *North American Review.* Here the author confesses that his grand design inevitably entailed sacrifices of this sort. "The book, however, critically viewed, is touchingly full of these disguised and repaired losses, these insidious recoveries, these intensely redemptive consistencies." A frank plea like this shows James's complex awareness of his own strength and weaknesses.

The Preface to *The Ambassadors* is indeed full of complexities. It illustrates as well as any other the important assertions R. P. Blackmur made of all James's prefaces: that no body of fiction is more suited to criticism than James's; that no author was better able to criticize his own work; that this preface serves particularly well to reveal the essential qualities, good and bad, of James's favorite work. "There is a contagion and a beautiful desolation," Blackmur concludes, "before

[20] See Oscar Cargill, *The Novels of Henry James* (New York, 1961), pp. 306–8.
[21] See S. Gorley Putt, *Henry James: A Reader's Guide* (Ithaca, 1966), pp. 358–59.

a great triumph of the human mind—before any approach to perfection—which we had best face for what there is in them." [22]

But fruitful and provocative as the Preface has proved over the years, it does not raise or settle all the critical issues readers have continued to raise about *The Ambassadors*. James's letters to friends like the Duchess of Sutherland and Hugh Walpole show him engaged still in explaining his book. If his Preface answers many important queries about the living source, the themes, the central propriety and some ancillary arrangements in the fictional method, it left other significant subjects unexplained and unexplored. Some of these are fundamental to a full understanding of this work. The novel's style and language, its imagery, the substratum of ideas or ideologies, its relation to James's other writings (especially to *The Wings of the Dove* and *The Golden Bowl*), and the place of *The Ambassadors* in the history of the modern novel in England and America—these are aspects of the novel explored beyond the limits of the Preface by such critics as Joan Bennett, Ian Watt, and U. C. Knoepflmacher.

Professor Watt's analysis of James's style as exemplified in the opening paragraph of *The Ambassadors* is a masterful example of sensitive reading. The fact that this exercise in close textual analysis did not appear until 1960 says something amusing and ironic about the practice of criticism in England and America as applied to the art of Henry James, one of the saints in the heaven of the New Critics. As we have had to wait until recently for definitive statements about the text, so have close studies of the novel's language and style been slow in appearing. Watt's description of the sober, abstract, expository, unsensuous prose James creates to express Strether's consciousness goes well beyond earlier efforts at detailed explication. His study supports no startlingly new reading of the novel, and many critics will agree with his placing *The Ambassadors* in the comic or humorous category. As he admits, Watt's work substantiates Constance Rourke's description in *American Humor* of James's typical "low-keyed humor of defeat." [23]

Metaphorical patterns and imagistic *motifs* are other aspects one would have thought critics to have exhausted long ago but which, in fact, only recently have been carefully examined in *The Ambassadors*. Austin Warren's discussion of James's symbolic imagery (reprinted in Leon Edel, ed., *Henry James: A Collection of Critical Essays*) offers

---

[22] *The Art of the Novel: Critical Prefaces by Henry James* (New York, 1946), p. xxxii.

[23] Among several valuable stylistic studies which have appeared since Watt's essay, the most successful is David Lodge's analysis of the opening paragraph of Chapter XXXI in *Language of Fiction: Essays in Criticism and Verbal Analysis* (London and New York, 1966), pp. 189–213.

the definitive statement of James's double mode of figuring human perceptions—the dialectic and the mythic. Though less purely than *The Wings of the Dove*, *The Ambassadors* exhibits the protagonist's initiation proceeding by metaphor as well as by close conversation. Certain facts and relationships are talked about, discovered cooperatively; other perceptions, more private and intuitive, can only be "imaged" or rendered emblematically. Oscar Cargill summarizes earlier critics in his discussion of the water-boat-iceberg-river cluster of images which, together with the Christian imagery associated with the Garden, form two chief *motifs*.[24] A third, closely associated pattern, which previous critics had noted but which U. C. Knoepflmacher develops most fully and convincingly, is the Shakespearean analogy to *Antony and Cleopatra* reprinted below. Even more than Watt's essay, Knoepflmacher's reinforces an ironic reading of Strether's whole experience. Such interpretations represent the current critical tendency to come down hard on the word "comically" as the decisive note struck by Maria Gostrey when on the last page of *The Ambassadors* she "sighed it at last all comically, all tragically, away."

The importance of ideas—political, social, aesthetic, philosophical, even theological—as such is a matter James says nothing about in the Preface to *The Ambassadors*. Since Strether's story is unique, in the fullest sense the study of one consciousness and one set of relationships, many readers have resisted seeing the relevance of any general ideas or ideologies to the novel. As T. S. Eliot put it tersely: "James did not provide us with 'ideas' but with another world of thought and feeling."[25] Joan Bennett's essay offers a cogent defense of Eliot's thesis. Others, however, noting the abstract and universal tendencies of James's style and of Strether's mind, have found in *The Ambassadors* identifiable and significant reflections of the intellectual milieu of James's day. For these critics, the James family provides the chief source or channel through which European or American institutions or schools of thought reach the novel. Emersonian idealism, the pragmatism of William James (especially as linked to British empiricism), and the peculiar Swedenborgian mysticism of Henry James, Sr., are three formulations which have provided interesting new interpretations of James's fiction, including *The Ambassadors*.[26] More inclusively, R. P. Blackmur has discussed the "precarious but precious

[24] *The Novels of Henry James*, pp. 325-27.
[25] "A Prediction," reprinted in Leon Edel, ed., *Henry James: A Collection of Critical Essays*, p. 56.
[26] See especially Eliseo Vivas, "Henry and William (Two Notes)," *Kenyon Review*, V (Autumn, 1943), 580-94; F. O. Matthiessen, *The James Family* (New York, 1947), 673-84; John H. Raleigh, "Henry James: The Poetics of Empiricism," *PMLA*,

place" ideas occupy in James's imagination. His essay, reprinted here, is a succinct statement of the novel's place in the intellectual history of the "disinherited sensibility"; it enlarges the scope of Miss Bennett's argument without destroying her conclusions. John H. Raleigh points up the issues to be faced in this area. "The critical problems," he writes, "are, first, to find James' Aquinas, or the rationale for the body of ideas on which the late novels constitute a metaphor, and, second, to define the relationship between this logical statement and James' symbolic one." [27]

Efforts in this direction, even if derided by minds as eminent as Eliot's, do serve at least to clarify some important linkages among James's three late works. *The Ambassadors, The Wings of the Dove,* and *The Golden Bowl* have manifestly so much in common that they have usually (if loosely) been referred to as a trilogy. Christof Wegelin provides a typical rationale: all are works in which international contrasts serve as the forum for fine moral discriminations; all are stylistically distinguishable from the earlier James; together they form a thematic progression in the experience of the chief character—initiation (Strether), conversion (Merton Densher), and fusion (Maggie Verver). Other parallels and progressions have been observed by, among others, Stephen Spender, Austin Warren, R. P. Blackmur, Frederick C. Crews, Quentin Anderson, Sister M. Corona Sharp.[28] Nearly all readers concur in noting the increasing predominance of myth over dialectic in these three fairytale narratives which become progressively more dense in metaphor and symbolism as social realities fade into the background. Such common features and patterns of development lead most critics to conclude that *The Ambassadors* is one of three works which, if not narrowly a trilogy, are more closely tied together than any others of James's works. Moreover, full comprehension of any one demands comparison of all three.

Most final judgments about Henry James's contribution to the novel turn on the premise that his three late works are indeed the novelist's culminating achievement. Walter Allen's is a representative, if enthusiastic, summation:

LXVI, No. 2 (March, 1951), 107–23; and Quentin Anderson, *The American Henry James* (New Brunswick, 1957), *passim* but particularly pp. 207–31.

[27] "Henry James: The Poetics of Empiricism," p. 107.

[28] See Wegelin, *op. cit.,* pp. 87–88; also Spender, *The Destructive Element* (London, 1935); Warren, "Symbolic Imagery"; Blackmur, *The Literary History of the United States,* eds. Spiller, Thorp, Johnson, and Canby (New York, 1948), Chap. LXIII; Crews, *The Tragedy of Manners: Moral Drama in the Later Novels of Henry James* (New Haven, 1957), Chap. 2; Anderson, *The American Henry James,* pp. 208–31; Sister M. Corona Sharp, osu, *The Confidante in Henry James: Evolution and Moral Value of a Fictive Character* (Notre Dame, 1963), p. 180.

The final splendid flowering of James's genius came in these three last novels, *The Wings of the Dove* (1902), *The Ambassadors* (1903), and *The Golden Bowl* (1904), novels of a classical perfection never before achieved in English in which practice and theory are consummately matched.

   . . . We know James as a novelist better than any other apart from Flaubert, and in the history of the English novel James holds a position analogous to Flaubert's in the French; both strove to give the novel the aesthetic intensity of a great poem or a great painting.[29]

If James *is* better known "as a novelist" than other late-nineteenth-century novelists in English, it is partly because, late in his long career and at the height of his powers, his technical discoveries of narrative method and of symbolic language first found in *The Ambassadors* their "appropriate form." To say this is not, however, to resolve the problem of James's modernity which several of the essayists collected here debate. Whether he is more a nineteenth-century artist, operating still inside the conventions of Victorian fiction and within the limits of intelligence and logically ordered discourse, or whether he is one of the first moderns, frankly embracing fluidity, ambiguity, and radical relativity in the exploration of mental process, is still open to speculation in the case of a novel like *The Ambassadors*.

Moreover, Allen's comparison of James to Flaubert, flattering though it is, demonstrates the exotic relation many feel James bears to traditional English fiction. F. R. Leavis' well-known discriminations are shared by other critics and historians, and they make no room for *The Ambassadors*. Judged by the notion that the novel is essentially the expression of a critical (that is, an ethical) sensibility engaged in analyzing society "as a system of functions and responsibilities," the book is not actually an English novel, but something else. For as Leavis sees it, James late in his career substituted for his earlier "intense critical interest in civilization" a new set of concerns—an uncontrolled symbolism, a hypertrophy of technique, a romantic system of purely private values. *The Ambassadors* illustrates with painful clarity how completely James "lost touch with concrete life" and thereby cut himself off from the mainstream of British fiction.[30]

The force of Leavis' categorical exclusion drives poor Strether and his story in the direction of Richard Chase and his version of the traditional American romance. To be sure, *The Ambassadors* superficially bears faint resemblance to typical American works of fiction

---

[29] Walter Allen, *The English Novel: A Short Critical History* (New York, 1955), pp. 327, 311.
[30] See F. R. Leavis, *The Great Tradition* (London, 1948), *passim*, and *The Common Pursuit* (London, 1952), pp. 228–32.

like *The Deerslayer, Moby-Dick,* and *The Bear.* But at some deeper levels, perhaps, the links are stronger, and readers of *The American Novel and Its Tradition* may regret that Chase did not choose to examine James's later works in terms of his paradigmatic formula, which, after all, derives many of its categories from James's own Prefaces. Despite obvious and important differences in characterization, narrative method, and setting, *The Ambassadors* shares with other American novels certain common conceptions of the hero, his career in society, his fate. The solitary innocent whose "Adamic" actions often assume unreal or symbolic or melodramatic form, whose mind plays games with ordinary experience, and whose moral imagination finally impels him to take visual but not actual possession of his world, is a type of the American hero. His names have been many—Natty Bumppo, Miles Coverdale, Ishmael, Pierre Glendinning, Huck Finn, Jay Gatsby, Ike McCaslin, among others. Lambert Strether might be astonished to find himself ranged in such a polyglot pantheon; we may imagine him playing his eternal nippers about on the company in mock dismay. But the affinities are there, as they are also for Christopher Newman, Isabel Archer, and Milly Theale. These creatures of James's imagination are all romantics set down in a real world which they proceed to try to transform. The shape of their experience, as Chase demonstrates in his analysis of *The Portrait of a Lady,* fits both the pattern of the novel and the romance in a manner recognizably American.[31]

Literary-historical generalizations like Allen's, Leavis', and Chase's are at best imprecise tools for describing individual works. If *The Ambassadors* evades their categories and remains stubbornly a Jamesian rather than a Continental, English, or American novel, this fact merely reinforces our realization of the ultimate individuality of all works of art. A critical method like James's own—"nothing, ever, but appreciation of the thing criticised"—will perhaps serve better than more doctrinaire approaches to isolate and judge the quiddity of *The Ambassadors.*

Assuredly the essays collected here do not say all. Neither do the additional books and essays listed in the Selected Bibliography. Many important issues remain for the reader to decide for himself. Three of the most persistent are these: the proportions of sympathy and irony in James's treatment of all the major characters, but especially of Strether; the consistency of Strether's final act of renunciation and withdrawal (Is it actually the outgrowth of character or does it follow too categorically the dictates of James's plot?); and, finally and most

---

[31] See Richard Chase, *The American Novel and Its Tradition* (Garden City, N.Y., 1957), pp. 21–28, 117–37.

fundamentally, the power of James's narrative method to catch and hold our sympathetic attention. This collection of viewpoints and interpretations should serve to redirect attention back to the text of *The Ambassadors* with renewed appreciation of its subtleties and complexities.

PART ONE

View Points

Henry James

Torquay, October 31st, 1895.

I was struck last evening with something that Jonathan Sturges, who has been staying here 10 days, mentioned to me: it was only 10 words, but I seemed, as usual, to catch a glimpse of a *sujet de nouvelle* in it. We were talking of W.D.H. and of his having seen him during a short and interrupted stay H. had made 18 months ago in Paris— called away—back to America, when he had just come—at the end of 10 days by the news of the death—or illness—of his father. He had scarcely been in Paris, ever, in former days, and he had come there to see his domiciled and initiated son, who was at the Beaux Arts. Virtually in the evening, as it were, of life, it was all new to him: all, all, all. Sturges said he seemed sad—rather brooding; and I asked him what gave him (Sturges) that impression. "Oh—some-where—I forget, when I was with him—he laid his hand on my shoulder and said *à propos* of some remark of mine: 'Oh, you are young, you are young—be glad of it: be glad of it and *live*. Live all you can: it's a mistake not to. It doesn't so much matter what you do—but live. This place makes it all come over me. I see it now. I haven't done so—and now I'm old. It's too late. It has gone past me—I've lost it. You have time. You are young. Live!' " I amplify and improve a little—but that was the tone. It touches me—I can see him—I can hear him. Immediately, of course—as everything, thank God, does—it suggests a little situation. I seem to see some-thing, of a tiny kind, springing out of it, that would take its place in the little group I should like to do of *Les Vieux*—The Old. (What should I call it in English—*Old Fellows*? No, that's trivial and com-mon.) At any rate, it gives me the little idea of the figure of an elderly man who hasn't "lived," hasn't at all, in the sense of sensations, passions, impulses, pleasures—and to whom, in the presence of some great human spectacle, some great organization for the Immediate, the

From The Notebooks of Henry James, *edited by F. O. Matthiessen and Kenneth B. Murdock (New York, 1947), pp. 225-28. Copyright 1947 by Oxford University Press, Inc. Reprinted by permission of the publisher.*

Agreeable, for curiosity, and experiment and perception, for Enjoyment, in a word, becomes, *sur la fin,* or toward it, sorrowfully aware. He has never really enjoyed—he has lived only for Duty and conscience—his conception of them; for pure appearances and daily tasks—lived for effort, for surrender, abstention, sacrifice. I seem to see his history, his temperament, his circumstances, his figure, his life. I don't see him as having battled with his passions—I don't see him as harassed by his temperament or as having, in the past, suspected, very much, what he was losing, what he was not doing. The alternative wasn't present to him. He may be an American—he might be an Englishman. I don't altogether like the *banal* side of the revelation of Paris—it's so obvious, so usual to make Paris the vision that opens his eyes, makes him feel his mistake. It might be London— it might be Italy—it might be the general impression of a summer in Europe—abroad. Also, it *may* be Paris. He has been a great worker, a local worker. But of what kind? I can't make him a novelist—too like W.D.H., and too generally *invraisemblable.* But I want him "intellectual," I want him *fine,* clever, literary almost: it deepens the irony, the tragedy. A clergyman is too obvious and *usé* and otherwise impossible. A journalist, a lawyer—these men WOULD in a manner have "lived," through their contact with life, with the complications and turpitudes and general vitality of mankind. A doctor—an artist too. A mere man of business—he's possible; but not of the intellectual grain that I mean. The Editor of a Magazine—that would come nearest: not at all of a newspaper. A Professor in a college would imply some knowledge of the lives of the young—though there might be a tragic effect in his seeing at the last that he hasn't even suspected what those lives might contain. (They had passed by him—he had passed them by.) He has married very young, and austerely. Happily enough, but charmlessly, and oh, so conscientiously: a wife replete with the New England conscience. But all this must be—oh, so light, so delicately summarized, so merely touched. What I seem to see is the possibility of some little illustrative action. The idea of the tale being the revolution that takes place in the poor man, the impression made on him by the particular experience, the incident in which this revolution and this impression embody themselves, is the point *à trouver.* They are determined by certain circumstances, and they produce a situation, his issue from which is the little drama. I am supposing him, I think, to have "illustrated," as I say, in the past, by his issue from some *other* situation, the opposite conditions, those that have determined him in the sense of the sort of life and feeling I have sketched and the memory, the consciousness of which roll over him now with force. He has sacrificed some one, some friend, some son, some younger brother, to his failure to feel, to understand, all that his new experience causes to come home to him in a wave of reaction, of compunction. He has not allowed for these things, the new things, new sources of emotion, new influences and appeals—didn't realize them at all. It was in communication with *them* that the spirit, the sense, the nature, the temperament of this victim (as now seems to him) of his old ignorance, struggled and suffered. He was wild—he was free—he was passionate; but there would have been a way of taking him. Our friend never saw it—never, never: he perceives that—ever so sadly, so bitterly, now. The young man is dead: it's all over. Was he a son, was he a ward, a younger brother—or an elder one? Points to settle: though I'm not quite sure I like the *son*. Well, my vague little fancy is that he "comes out," as it were (to London, to Paris—I'm afraid it *must* be Paris; if he's an American), to take some step, decide some question with regard to some one, in the sense of his old feelings and habits, and that the new influences, to state it roughly, make him act just in the opposite spirit—make him accept on the spot, with a *volte-face*, a wholly different inspiration. It is a case of some other person or persons, it is some other young life in regard to which it's a question of his interfering, rescuing, bringing home. Say he "goes out" (partly) to look after, to bring home, some young man whom his family are anxious about, who won't *come* home, etc.—and under the operation of the change *se range due côté du jeune homme*, says to him: "No; STAY:—*don't* come home." Say our friend is a widower, and that the *jeune homme* is the son of a widow to whom he is engaged to be married. *She* is of the strenuous pattern—she is the reflection of his old self. She has money—she admires and approves him: 5 years have elapsed since his 1st wife's death, 10 since his own son's. He is 55. He married at 20! Displeasing the strenuous widow is a sacrifice—an injury to him. To marry her means rest and security *pour ses vieux jours*. The "revolution" endangers immensely his situation with her. But of course my denouement is that it takes place—that he makes the sacrifice, does the thing I have, vaguely, represented him, *supra*, as doing, and loses the woman he was to marry and all the advantages attaching to her. It is too late, too late *now*, for HIM to live—but what stirs in him with a dumb passion of desire, of I don't know what, is the sense that he may have a little supersensual hour in the vicarious freedom of another. His little drama is the administration of the touch that contributes to—that prolongs—that freedom.

Letter from James to the Duchess of Sutherland

Rye, Dec. 23rd, 1903.

Take, meanwhile pray, the *Ambassadors* very easily and gently:
read five pages a day—be even as deliberate as that—but *don't break
the thread.* The thread is really stretched quite scientifically tight.
Keep along with it step by step—and then the full charm will come
out. I *want* the charm, you see, to come out for you—so convinced
am I that it's there! Besides, I find that the very most difficult thing
in the art of the novelist is to give the impression and illusion of
the real *lapse of time, the quantity* of time, represented by our poor
few phrases and pages, and all the drawing-out the reader can contribute helps a little perhaps the production of that spell.

From The Selected Letters of Henry James, *edited by Leon Edel (Garden City,
N.Y., 1960), p. 190. Reprinted by permission of Farrar, Straus & Giroux, Inc.*

Review in *The Nation*

The Ambassadors. By Henry James. Harper & Brothers.

In many of Mr. James's novels Americans abroad are important
figures, but it is long since he has permitted his wandering compa-
triots to occupy the scene so exclusively as they do in "The Ambassadors." The superficial differences between Americans and Eu-
ropeans, so sharply defined in his earlier books, are in his latest
one but lightly indicated; yet an enduring fundamental difference
of natural outlook and attitude towards life is much more elaborately
and profoundly studied. Thus, there is a tacit recognition of a
modification of American asperities, or, at least, peculiarities, wrought
by a generation of pretty intimate association with peoples whose
manners are as good as, perhaps better than, their morals.

The Ambassadors in Paris excite neither curiosity nor surprise by
their outward seeming, and something more than mere acquaintance would be necessary for a Parisian to discover the abiding for-
eignness of the inward breast. What comes out strongly in the earlier
books is the effect, the upsetting effect, produced on Europe by Amer-

From The Nation, *LXXVIII (February 4, 1904), 95. The review was written by
Annie R. M. Logan.*

icans, their looks, their ways, and their money; but the great thing in the latest one is the effect of Europe, specifically of Paris, on the Ambassadors—the way Woollett standards of thought, of conduct, even of abstract right and wrong, are, temporarily at least, infected and impaired by actual agreeable contact with the way things are thought and felt and done in Paris.

Chad Newsome, during a prolonged voluntary exile from Woollett, took on a wonderful exotic air. The chief Ambassador, Lambert Strether, meeting Chad at the opera, is amazed at the ease, the grace, the external perfection of one whom he remembered as looking bold and wild. But as soon as Strether penetrates the surface, he recognizes his own; he knows that this dazzling vision is "only Chad," to which incontrovertible fact, sometime, far off perhaps, but surely in the end, Mme. de Vionnet would be sacrificed. The mission of Strether, who has issued forth from Woollett with credentials from an anxious mother, is to investigate Chad, to find out what sinister influences keep him in Paris, deaf to repeated maternal calls for his return. Strether is empowered to remonstrate with Chad, to cajole, to threaten, to bring him, no matter by what means, back to Woollett, to the flourishing industry which he has inherited and which, with the benefit of his administration, is destined to become even more flourishing. The mission of the subsequent Ambassadors, Chad's own sister, Sarah, and her husband, Jim Pocock, is to find out what keeps Strether in Paris, to call him to account for neglect of official duty, for comprehensive failure, both as an ambassador and as a man once thought worthy of Mrs. Newsome's confidence, with whom she had gone so far as to express a willingness to share her declining years and the fortune of the late Mr. Newsome.

Woollett has always supposed that the sinister influence holding Chad in bondage is female—a supposition soon verified by Strether; but the verification, the recognition of some sort of a binding relation between Chad and Mme. de Vionnet doesn't help Strether to do his duty; it only provides him with confusing impressions, with endless contrasting and conflicting thoughts, feelings, and speculations, all serving rather to emphasize the wrongness of Woollett's judgment than the correctness of its gross suspicions. There had probably never been a time when Strether could have shuffled off a moral inheritance with the clever cynicism of his ambiguous cicerone, Miss Gostrey, or the indifference of the all-wise "Little Bilham." No! he could never have said, Evil be thou my good. At all events, the opportunity to deny his fathers' gods came too late. At fifty-five the best and the worst he could get out of Paris was a feast for a starved impressionability, a sensation from a woman of inexpressible charm which lifted her above the censure of Woollett, shamed the purpose of the embassy, and almost cast a halo round the treason of the ambassador. Sarah Pocock let him know that he had been guilty of treason and made short work of the halo. Chad had tried to divert Sarah from her mission, from his own delinquency and Strether's, by treating the Pocock minatory expedition as if it were a family pleasure party. But though the lady graciously accepted attention, and though Jim succumbed at once, Strether knew in his guilty heart "that treating her handsomely buttered no parsnips; and that in fine there were moments when she felt the fixed eyes of her admirable, absent mother fairly screw into the flat of her back." On the day when the screw touched her marrow, she fell upon Strether. She put it to him straight—all the culpability of his condonation of Chad's hideous conduct; all the weakness of his surrender to Mme. de Vionnet and the blackness of his defence of that person, "when the most distinguished woman we shall either of us have seen in this world [Sarah's admirable mother] sits there insulted in her loneliness by your incredible comparison." Thus did Sarah sweep the cobwebs from Strether's brain, and force him to suspect that Chad's relation with Mme. de Vionnet involved an irreconcilable difference between Woollett and Paris. When he came more clearly to perceive how much he had been caught in a net, how much, perhaps, bamboozled by delicacy and grace conceivable only in the blameless, he understood at least that he was inevitably and by the nature of things committed to Woollett, and that he must go back to its dulness and its decency, its (humanly speaking) ghastly emptiness.

In the course of the story Strether asks "Little Bilham" a pointed question about Chad and the De Vionnets, mother and daughter. "I can only tell you," answers that youthful master of equivocation, "that it's what they pass for. But isn't that enough? What more than a vain appearance does the wisest of us know? I commend you the vain appearance." This answer suggests the substance of what seems to be Mr. James's theory of realistic representation. He strives constantly for the vain appearance. His plan of campaign is to show how an incident or train of incidents appears to one or two or twenty people, what each makes out of the complication, and how his interpretation affects his feeling, judgment, conduct. In life nobody ever knows (except by direct revelation or accident) the truth about anybody else, or exactly understands a situation in which he is not directly involved. But we are all always interested observers of other people, very keen about their affairs, guessing, implying, inferring. By delineating interested observers thus pleasantly engrossed in an interesting situation, Mr. James tries for very extended realistic representation, and very difficult, because part of his task is, through his various readings of the vain appearance, to show the truth, or, at least, to indicate the greater probability. In "The Ambassadors" he permits an accident to reveal to Strether coldly and hardly a truth about which in the gray after years of Woollett he might have contrived to entertain a solacing doubt. We regret so definite a declaration, not only for poor dear Strether's sake, but also because it somewhat discredits a theory so admirably justified up to that point. After Sarah Pocock's onslaught, all the impressions are recorded, all the evidence is in. Strether and any readers who might still waver about a verdict should, we think, have had the chance. For ourselves, the vain appearance suffices, and we therefore offer for contemplation a possibly grave, certainly new, fault in Mr. James—that of having been too explicit.

Letter from James to Hugh Walpole

Lamb House, Rye, Aug. 14th, 1912.

. . . It's charming to me to hear that *The Ambassadors* have again engaged and still beguile you; it *is* probably a very *packed* production, with a good deal of one thing within another; I remember sitting on it, when I wrote it, with that intending weight and presence with which you probably often sit in these days on your trunk to make the lid close and *all* your trousers and boots go in. I remember putting in a good deal about Chad and Strether, or Strether and Chad, rather; and am not sure that I quite understand what in that connection you miss—I mean in the way of what *could* be there. The whole thing is of course, to intensity, a picture of relations—and among them is, though not on the first line, the relation of Strether to Chad. The relation of Chad to Strether is a limited and according to my method only implied and indicated thing, sufficiently there; but Strether's to Chad consists above all in a charmed and yearning and wondering sense, a dimly envious sense, of all Chad's young living and easily-taken *other* relations; other not only than the one to him, but than the one to Mme de Vionnet and whoever else; this very sense, and the sense of Chad, generally, is a part, a large part, of poor dear Strether's discipline, development, adventure and general history. All of it that is of my subject seems to me given—given by dramatic projection, as all the rest is given: how can you say I do anything so foul and abject

as to "state"? You deserve that I should condemn you to read the book
over once again!

Arnold Bennett

Artistic prestige has an influence not only on my blood-vessels but
on my critical faculty. It took me years to ascertain that Henry James's
work was giving me little pleasure. I first had a glimpse of the distress-
ing fact when "What Masie knew" began to appear serially in *The
New Review* ages ago—somewhere in the Ninth Dynasty. By the one
thousand persons (including myself) in England who are genuinely
interested in the art of literature, this serial was anticipated with a religious eagerness. I could not get on with it. My fault, of course. Impossible to credit that anything of Henry James was not great! But
when I was immovably bogged in the middle of "The Golden Bowl,"
and again in the middle of "The Ambassadors" (supposed, both of
them, to mark the very summit of Henry James's achievement) I grew
bolder with myself. In each case I asked myself: "What the dickens is
this novel *about,* and where does it think it is going to?" Question
unanswerable! I gave up.

At this present I have no recollection whatever of any character or
any event in either novel. And I will venture to say that I have honestly
enjoyed, and been held by only two of James's novels: "In the Cage,"
and "The Other House." The former is very short, and the later is not
interminable.

I am willing to admit, for the sake of argument, that Henry James
knew more about the technique of the novel than any other novelist
(save Turgenev). He was fond of saying that a novel, to be aristically
satisfactory, must be "organised"; and he "organised" his own with
unique and inhuman elaboration. I will also admit, without any re-
serve, that his style, though unduly mannered, is very distinguished,
and that he said what he so subtly meant with unsurpassed accuracy.
I will admit that he knew everything about writing novels—except
how to keep my attention.

My doubt is whether he had actually much to say in a creative sense,
that needed saying. I think that he knew a lot about the life of one
sort of people, the sort who are what is called cultured, and who do
themselves very well both physically and intellectually; and very little

From The Savour of Life *by Arnold Bennett. Copyright 1928 by Doubleday &
Company, Inc. Reprinted by permission of Doubleday & Company, Mrs. Dorothy
Cheston Bennett, and Cassell & Co. Ltd.*

indeed about life in general. I think that in the fastidiousness of his taste he rather repudiated life.

He was a man without a country. He never married. He never, so far as is commonly known, had a love-affair worthy of the name. And I would bet a fiver that he never went into a public-house and had a pint of beer—or even half a pint. He was naïve, innocent, and ignorant of fundamental things to the last. He possessed taste, but his taste lacked robustness. He had the most delicate perceptions: but he perceived things with insufficient emotion. He was mostly afraid of being vulgar, and even of being carried away. My notion is that most first-rate creative artists simply do not know what vulgarity is. They go right on, and if it happens to them to be vulgar in the stresses of creation, well, it happens to them—and they are forgiven.

Yvor Winters

This moral sense, as it existed about equally in James and in his characters, then, was a fine, but a very delicate perception, unsupported by any clear set of ideas, and functioning, not only in minds of very subtle construction, but at the very crisis in history at which it was doomed not only to be almost infinitely rarefied but finally to be dissolved in air. Since James conceived the art of the novel primarily in terms of plot, and plot almost wholly in terms of ethical choice and of its consequences; since he raised the plotting of the novel to a level of seriousness which it had never before attained in English; since all intelligent criticism of James is resolved inevitably into a discussion of plot; this moral sense, this crisis in history, will prove, I believe, to be the source of the essential problem of James's art.

*   *   *

If we proceed from these latter works to the latest, and consider the book which for James was his most satisfactory, *The Ambassadors*, we have at least three sources of difficulty, of possible dissatisfaction. In the first place, it is only by stretching a point that we can bring ourselves to consider Chad Newsome at best a bone worth quite so much contention, worth the expenditure of quite so much moral heroism as Strether expends upon him. We can understand Chad's hesitation to return to the American business life of his period, but his alternative—

From Maule's Curse: Seven Studies in the History of American Obscurantism *by Yvor Winters (Norfolk, Conn., 1938). Reprinted in* In Defense of Reason, (*Swallow Press, Chicago, copyright 1947*), *pp. 306, 334–35. Reprinted by permission of The Swallow Press, Incorporated.*

that of a young man about Paris, however cultivated,—is scarcely the alternative of a Henry Adams. The central issue does not quite support the dramatics, as does, on the other hand, the central issue of each of the other late masterpieces, *The Golden Bowl* and *The Wings of the Dove.* Furthermore, our final attitude toward Chad is unresolved, and thus resembles our final attitude toward Owen Gereth in *The Spoils of Poynton;* this may not be untrue to life, but it is untrue to art, for a work of art is an evaluation, a judgment, of an experience, and only in so far as it is that is it anything; and James in this one respect does not even judge the state of uncertainty, but as in *The Spoils of Poynton,* he merely leaves us uncertain. Shakespeare left us in no uncertainty about Coriolanus; Melville in none about Ahab or Benito Cereno; nor did either author lack subtlety. And finally, Strether's ultimate scruple—to give up Maria Gostrey, so that he may not seem in Woollett to have got anything for himself from a situation in which he will seem to his friends in Woollett to have betrayed his trust, and in spite of the fact that Miss Gostrey could scarcely have been regarded as in any sense a bribe—this scruple, I say, impresses me very strongly as a sacrifice of morality to appearances: there might, conceivably, have been more Christian humility in considering the feelings of Maria Gostrey and in letting his reputation in Woollett go by the board. The moral choice, here, appears to be of the same strained and unjustifiable type as that of Fleda Vetch, or as that of Isabel Archer.

Elizabeth Stevenson

One should remember, too, that victimization works both ways. The most triumphant turnabout of this theme is the story of Chad Newsome and Marie de Vionnet in *The Ambassadors.* In this novel the young American is the cruel exploiter, and the older, experienced European woman is the gentle victim. . . .

Victimization is only the obvious face of the story. Other, more knowing Americans go abroad with brave intentions. Europe, as the complex of thickness representing "life" for James, proves too much for the talented, the intelligent, and the good. The artist Roderick Hudson chokes on the quantity of inspiration available in Rome; Isabel chooses the wrong husband out of a superfluity of applicants

From The Crooked Corridor: A Study of Henry James *by Elizabeth Stevenson* (*New York, 1949*), *pp. 60–61. Copyright 1949 by The Macmillan Company. Reprinted by permission of the publisher.*

who offer themselves to her in England and in Italy; and Maggie finds the worst fortune enshrined in what had seemed unbeatable felicity.

Below the tragicomedy of misunderstanding and misjudgment in these national contrasts and clashes is a profound theme. James' American in Europe is attempting to complete himself, to find a fit extension of the self in the outer world. He is a person searching for a habitation. Yet his native freedom makes him one who breaks the mold to which he is trying to adapt himself. He finds out its cracks and flaws as easily as Maggie finds the fault in the golden bowl.

The movement from America to Europe has different names for each individual: for Newman it signifies the exchange of barrenness for profusion; for Isabel, the exchange of ignorance for knowledge; for Lambert Strether, the exchange of Puritanism for a sense of joy.

He, the middle-aged hero of *The Ambassadors,* is almost the best, as he is almost the last, of James' American heroes. He has the damning gift of a moral sense that is identical with his imagination.

E. K. Brown

Perhaps it was from Turgenev that Henry James learned the art of arranging characters by gradation and combining with it surprise. It is James's mastery of gradation that E. M. Forster is neglecting when he complains of the fewness of the types of character that furnish the novels of James. "He has," says Forster, "a very short list of characters. . . . the observer who tries to influence the action, and the second-rate outsider. . . . Then there is the sympathetic foil, very lively and frequently female . . . there is the wonderful rare heroine . . . there is sometimes a villain, sometimes a young artist with generous impulses; and that is about all. For so fine a novelist it is a poor show." It is a short list; but is it a poor show?

In *The Ambassadors,* the novel Mr. Forster examines, there is a young artist with generous impulses, Little Bilham, who has left America to study in Paris. In and about the ateliers he discovers that he has no talent for art, but a distinguished faculty for enjoying artistic and civilized company, the kind of company that Henry James preferred to that of poets and philosophers and would have preferred to that of archangels if he had believed in them. Little Bilham sets his course so that his distinguished faculty may develop and be exercised;

From Rhythm in the Novel *by E. K. Brown (Toronto, 1950), pp. 24–27. Copyright 1950 by the University of Toronto Press. Reprinted by permission of the publisher.*

he has the dignity of self-knowledge and simple consistency. As the observer who tries to influence the action—in *The Ambassadors* this is Lambert Strether, the elderly New Englander—approaches a building in the Boulevard Malesherbes, he sees Little Bilham smoking on a balcony. He had hoped he might see another young man, Chad Newsome, whose balcony this is, and whom it is Strether's mission to rescue from the wickedness of Europe and ship home to his mother and the manufacturing town of Woollett, Massachusetts. Strether has not seen Chad for over five years; but he quickly appreciates that much as Chad may have changed he cannot have changed so much as to have become the little man on the balcony. For the rest of the novel we are invited to measure Chad by Little Bilham. At first the comparison is all to Chad's advantage. Of the two young men who have come to Paris from America and enjoy there the best of artistic and civilized company, Chad seems by so much the more impressive. He is charming to look at; he is at the centre of the company, and Little Bilham seems only a permitted attendant spirit; and above all it is Chad who is loved by the rare and wonderful heroine of the novel, Madame de Vionnet. Chad has it all his own way. But we begin to make disturbing discoveries about Chad. He has not the dignity of self-knowledge, or the simple consistency of Little Bilham; he has been refined and polished by Madame de Vionnet, but the material was not of the first order, and the polish and refinement are not durable—they chip off. The appeal of the large sums of money to be made at Woollett grows stronger; and Chad grows tired of Madame de Vionnet, for with her he is living above his natural level. His shortcomings, his confusions, his inconsistencies appear in a scene that comes near the end of the novel, a scene on the same balcony of the building in the Boulevard Malesherbes. Strether and he come to grips smoking there; and the reader is helped to see what is amiss in Chad by his memory of the figure that had stood smoking on that balcony when Strether approached it for the first time.

There is gradation no less effective in the relationship between Chad and Strether. At first they appear totally unlike: the only things they have in common are their roots in New England, their respect for Mrs. Newsome and relation to her, and their presence in Paris. Strether responds with a gradual intensity to the appeal of the artistic and civilized company; and beginning as Mrs. Newsome's ambassador, urging Chad to sail for home, he shifts to become Madame de Vionnet's ambassador, urging him to stay in Paris. He becomes Chad's peer in the appreciation of Europe, and then his superior. He achieves Little Bilham's self-knowledge and simple consistency.

Each of these persons irradiates the others, and each becomes clearer by irradiation. By this irradiation the Jamesian scene assumes the soft contours of life that Thackeray achieved by his beautiful flexibility. The groupings of characters by gradation enables James to draw from that "short list" of his a show that is very far from being a poor one. James's rhythmic use of gradation does not make for strength and boldness as Turgenev's does, but the strength and boldness come from his complementary use of antithesis—Mrs. Newsome set over against Madame de Vionnet, Waymarsh the American success set over against Gloriani the European success, Mamie Pocock the nubile girl of the American ruling class versus Jeanne de Vionnet the perfect *jeune fille.*

F. W. Dupee

James believed *The Ambassadors* to be his most perfect novel; and certainly it boasts his most perfect plot, certainly it gathers up into a powerful design all his major themes. If he drew on Howells for Strether's sentiments, he drew far more on himself: his European residence, his bachelor status, his writer's relation to his audience. There are more beauty and horror in *The Wings of the Dove* and *The Golden Bowl;* but *The Ambassadors* is mainly comedy, as they are not, and its attractions are the appropriate ones of grace and clarity. Nothing is developed at the expense of anything else; the novel means many things but they are all consonant with one another. Even when Strether refuses Maria Gostrey, he is not "renouncing" in the sometimes awkward way of James's heroes; he is only conceding frankly to the actualities of his mind, heart, and time of life. Like James during his Paris stay of years ago, he has given much of himself to the world; but he has retained his original faith in the primacy of spirit; and he has done this in order that he may survive as an entity and have a self to give. True, Strether's innocence is of the kind usually reserved for the fools or dupes of comedy. In refusing to draw this conclusion, in making Strether entirely charming, James risked perpetrating a fable *for* provincials as well as about them. His fears, as expressed in his notes, that Strether might cloy were partly justified; and Mme. de Vionnet, observed as she is so exclusively from without, tends to go stiff under the weight of all her representative grandeur.

These are casual defects in a book that remains an uncommonly persuasive whole. The wholeness is felt in a variety of ways. There is

From Henry James: His Life and Writings *by F. W. Dupee (Garden City, N.Y., 1956), pp. 214–15. Reprinted by permission of William Morrow & Co., Inc. Copyright © 1951 by William Sloane Associates, Inc.*

the sheer momentum of the action, which, among James's large efforts in the "scenic" kind, is unique in its steady advance towards an irresistible conclusion. The capacity, moreover, of his characters to throw light on one another, to enter into meaningful (and diverting!) relationships, is here carried as far as James was ever to carry it. We begin by noting the interesting symmetry made by Mrs. Newsome, Maria Gostrey, and Mme. de Vionnet; or by Strether, Jim Pocock, and the angular old Yankee, Waymarsh, Strether's occasional companion in Europe. But everyone in the novel, as we soon realize, is vitally connected with everyone else and there is no end of "foils." Finally there is the supremely successful setting—successful because so thoroughly subdued to the purposes of the novel. As distinguished from bourgeois Woollett, Strether's Paris is a city exclusively of artists and members of the nobility united in the pursuit of pleasure, enlightenment, and artistic creation. A place of fine surfaces, Paris is nevertheless seen to contain a mystery, a something that is at first merely postulated—it lurks behind that high window observed from the street or in those animated streets observed from a balcony. Then by degrees Strether penetrates the mystery: at the party in the secluded urban garden, over luncheon with Mme. de Vionnet in a quayside restaurant, in her drawingroom dense with suggestions of the First Empire and beyond. Indeed, this room is for him the ultimate Parisian interior, and there, during his final interview with a Mme. de Vionnet ravaged and diminished by her love for Chad, he remembers Mme. Roland and the guillotine, feels the tragic French passion behind the great French elegance, and sees what Woollett in its idealism refuses to see: the amount of sheer sacrifice, the blood and tears, entailed in the perpetuation of any culture worth the name.

F. R. Leavis

I may be wrong in this general suggestion, but I am sure that his commentary on *The Ambassadors* implies an indefensible valuation. Why should he assume that the reader tends, almost irresistibly (though mistakenly) to identify himself with Strether? I can only comment that I haven't been in the least tempted so to identify myself, or to spend any moral or intellectual energy determining the worth or significance of Strether's resolution to "have got nothing for him-

From The Common Pursuit *by F. R. Leavis (London, 1952, 1963), pp. 225–26. Reprinted by permission of the author, Chatto & Windus, Ltd., and the New York University Press.*

self." For all the light Mr. Anderson throws on possible intentions, *The Ambassadors* still seems to me so feeble a piece of word-spinning that I should have been inclined to dismiss it as merely senile if James hadn't himself provided an explanation in telling us that it had been conceived as a short story. What Mr. Anderson points to is a set of preoccupations that helps us to understand how James should have been so mistakenly led into fluffing out the story to the bulk and pretensions of a major work.

I suspect that *The Ambassadors,* which to me remains wholly boring, doesn't belong so essentially with the other late "great" novels as Mr. Anderson thinks—and as, perhaps, James himself in elaborating it, intended.

Wayne Booth

—If art were "for art's sake" in the limited sense of existing only to give pleasure through abstract forms and patternings, one would expect that a quest for one truth would be just as good as another, that the way in which the quest is formed would be the only important distinction between good and bad. Why should James not be able to write as great a book on the theme of *The Sacred Fount* as on that of *The Ambassadors?* The quest of a male gossip for a clear picture of the amatory pairings of a group of weekend guests is simply not as important as the quest of Strether for the meaning of life itself. Even if, by some miracle of will, James had been able to bring himself to develop *The Sacred Fount* with anything like the fulness of *The Ambassadors,* it would take another miracle of our wills to make us care about the first quest as much as the second. But the conflict between full consciousness and narrow conscience shown in *The Ambassadors* is something which everyone experiences, whether he knows it or not, and the novelist who can portray the conflict vividly will involve us in a quest close to our hearts.[1]

Strether was not the first hero to seek ethical truth that would re-

---

From The Rhetoric of Fiction *by Wayne Booth (Chicago, 1961), pp. 292–93. Reprinted by permission of the University of Chicago Press.*

[1] What I am saying here is true, of course, only so long as we are talking about works the primary interest of which is the intellectual quest for some kind of truth or vision. It should go without saying that a great comedy could be written about the quest of a male gossip for a clear picture of the amatory pairings of a group of weekend guests. James at times approaches this kind of comedy in *The Sacred Fount,* but he approaches it only to shift back into something else, something that seems to be trying for profundity and that in the trying ruins itself.

solve a conflict between conventional or superficial values. But he presages many works which, by removing the traditional certainties that might be provided in a play, heighten the reader's sense of the character's isolation as he faces his moral problems and thus heighten the reader's own dilemma as he reads. The reliable narrator of an older work like *Great Expectations* could provide a secure haven for the erring Pip, but there is no secure haven for Paul Morel or Stephen Dedalus. In this respect as in so many others, modern fiction has tried to move closer to life itself than was ever attempted by earlier fiction. Leave the reader to choose for himself, force him to face each decision as the hero faces it, and he will feel much more deeply the value of the truth when it is attained, or its loss if the hero fails.

PART TWO

Interpretations

Full Prime

by Joseph Warren Beach

It is characteristic of James that his best work of all should have come at the end of his career. His was an art that had to be learned. It is in the first decade of the present century that we reach the period of his richest self-expression. Having mastered his technique, having done with experiments, he launches at last upon that series of novels which are but the natural and seemingly unstudied application of his method, and the best demonstration of its possibilities for art.

We need not go over again the several points and show how they are applied in these novels. What does invite us is the opportunity of re-marking on the beautiful fruits of this method. It is in "The Dove," "The Ambassadors" and "The Golden Bowl" that we taste most those esthetic gratifications which only such a system can procure us. These are all structures of generous dimensions; and they are in no case over-crowded with tenants, who have thus ample room to turn around and ample leisure to make themselves at home. In other words, the process of selection and elimination makes possible the fullest and most faith-ful treatment of what is included. The central idea is allowed to grow as steady and unhampered as some great elm in New England fields, reaching out on all sides to the sun, and showing at last dense-foliaged and round, broad and symmetrical in its green acre. Each particular situation, or historical passage, which is deemed worthy of treatment at all, receives the same full-rounded development; each process in the consciousness of the characters, chosen for illustration or for intrinsic interest, is followed closely from step to step through all its course without abruptness, haste or violence. This smooth progress, free from jolts and jars, is a marked feature of the work of James in general, distinguishing it from the type of fiction that ministers to our love of

"*Full Prime*" by Joseph Warren Beach. *From* The Method of Henry James *(New Haven, 1918), pp. 255–56, 258–59, 260–62, 266–70. Copyright © 1918 by Yale Univer-sity Press. Reprinted by permission of the publisher.*

rapid movement, variety and change. James has naturally a predilection for slow movement, inappreciable change, for neat articulation and orderly evolution. He prefers likeness to difference, the familiar to the novel, since in each case the former has actually more to yield to the understanding, is more readily assimilated and made a part of one's total impression.

The amplitude of the record gives room for the carrying out of those large operations, or manœuvres, which amount to nothing less than a revolution in someone's life. Such an operation is not an affair like going to bed or taking breakfast, and is not to be disposed of in any light and cavalier fashion. It is a matter of long preparation, of many stages both in conception and execution. It has a logic and a sequence, which have to be followed throughout. In no part of James's work are there such fine examples of these operations extensively carried out as in these three late novels.

*   *   *

Such a large slow evolution again is, in "The Dove," the process by which Merton Densher gives himself up to the designs of Kate upon Milly, wandering farther and farther from the straight way, until the last momentous visit to the dying woman, where comes to a head the slow spirit of rebellion against a sinister manipulation, and he takes the sharp, decisive turn back to truth and decency. We need not trace out the course of this operation nor of that other performed by Strether in "The Ambassadors." The point is that only on this method, in this kind of novel, is it possible to conceive the execution of any such broad continuous figure. It is one thing to say, of such and such a change in a character's outlook, that it came about; it is another thing to give the reader the impression of its coming about. Every movement of the plot cries out for elbow-room. Each plot as a whole is like a fleet of warships demanding large waters in which to form and reform and go through their wide-sweeping manœuvres.

It is a double undertaking. The situations must be worked out completely in relation to the idea they make palpable; and they must be completely realized in scenes felt as real and particular human experience. Here again the leisurely fulness of treatment makes for our satisfaction. The situations grow upon us. Familiarity itself takes hold of us; and we are further convinced by the many little faithful touches, which are introduced as quietly as in life itself.

*   *   *

Another such occasion, to cite an example from "The Ambassadors," is that in which Strether, in his river-side pavilion, becomes aware of the presence of Chad and Madame de Vionnet in a row-boat, and of being himself discovered by the watchful eye of Madame de Vionnet. It takes indeed but two paragraphs to give an account of the moment that follows, but there is so much excitement crowded into this one moment of hesitation and suspense and the circumstances are so vividly imagined that we realize it as a complete little drama. We see the figures clearly in their physical relation and aspect,—Madame de Vionnet with her pink parasol shifted as if to hide her face, Chad in his shirt-sleeves and with his face turned away, having let his paddles go on receiving the mute warning of his companion, and poor Strether staring petrified in his pavilion. And we *feel* the tense indecision of the two in the boat, the horror of the gentleman on shore. It is of course the sensations of Strether that make the scene *live*.

It was a sharp fantastic crisis that had popped up as if in a dream, and it had had only to last the few seconds to make him feel it as quite horrible. They were thus, on either side, *trying* the other side, and all for some reason that broke the stillness like some unprovoked harsh note. It seemed to him again, within the limit, that he had but one thing to do—to settle their common question by some sign of surprise and joy. He hereupon gave large play to these things, agitating his hat and his stick and loudly calling out—a demonstration that brought him relief as soon as he had seen it answered. The boat, in mid-stream, still went a little wild—which seemed natural, however, while Chad turned round, half springing up; and his good friend, after blankness and wonder, began gaily to wave her parasol. Chad dropped afresh to his paddles and the boat headed round, amazement and pleasantry filling the air meanwhile, and relief, as Strether continued to fancy, superseding mere violence.[1]

In comparison with such work the narrative method of much of our most-admired fiction seems conventional and superficial. The characters are but lay-figures, hastily furnished with cloaks and swords, with legs and noses, from some theatrical wardrobe, and made to go through certain movements which, by a pious convention and the indulgence of the reader, are taken to mean action and emotion. Each situation is presented in merest outline, with no attempt at filling in those intimate touches that give reality to any situation and differentiate one situation from another. In James, we have the pleasure of seeing the figures grow and fill until they reach the rounded proportions of living beings. We watch the situation opening up, depth behind depth, with calculated distances and objects so placed as to give a sense of perspective. Whatever is undertaken is done, and we are satisfied.

But if James does impress us, in this ultimate work, with his ade-

[1] Vol. XXII, pp. 257-58.

quacy of treatment, that goes, as I have said, with the rigor of his elimination; and the very omissions contribute their element of beauty to the general effect. Certain surfaces are closely and finely covered, while others are left altogether blank, with the effect of wide significant margins. Their white spaces are something to rest and please the eye on their own account, as well as to give an accent to the shaded greys and blacks of the portions treated. There is given a pleasing sense of reserve-power, of fertile unbroken ground, particularly desirable for work that might otherwise incur the reproach of an excess of cultivation.

*   *   *

"The Ambassadors" has the distinction of being at once the simplest and the most complex in design of all the studies of James. It is simple in being an uninterrupted record of the intellectual adventure of one man in the exploration of one simple human situation. The problem of Strether draws its beautiful continuous line through the whole series of twelve books, a line gently and at last decidedly curving, yet never broken or obscured. But the study is at the same time complex or multiple in the number of aspects under which the subject may be viewed and named.

There is most obviously the particular problem of Chad Newsome, which forms the subject upon which the intelligence of Strether is perpetually exercised, and which determines the direction of all his "adventure." Yet I should hardly call this the subject of the book: it is too particular, too limited in its *portée*. The subject proper is something more abstract: it is the matter of free intellectual exploration in general, of the open mind in contrast to the mind closed and swaddled in prejudice and narrow views. Under another aspect this is seen to be again the inveterate contrast between the cosmopolitan and the provincial, between the European and the American outlook. Strether's discovery of the open mind is his discovery of Europe. It is Europe that teaches him how many and how delicate considerations are involved in the solution of his problem,—how much depends on facts and "values" not to be lightly determined in advance. And if it is Europe that stands here for the open mind, this Europe is more specifically embodied in the most cosmopolitan of cities.

Which makes it possible to say that the subject of this study is Paris. It is Paris that gives its particular tone and color to this work. It is hard to determine the respective parts in producing this effect of Paris material and Paris spiritual. If the predominance of white in this picture and the special quality of the white always bring to mind the color of Manet, it may well be our own impressions of the physical

city upon which the author draws largely for his effect. His descrip-
tions are no more extended, I think, than is usual in the later novels,
but we cannot escape the insistent note of this background, which is
always so vividly and yet discreetly present. The high balconies over
animated streets, the cheerful interiors of restaurant and café, domes-
tic interiors in varied but ever exquisite taste, the more stagey *décor*
of church and theatre, the light open spaces of *place* and *quai,* all
keep us reminded of the physical brightness and amenity of Paris.

But one can hardly distinguish background and foreground. There
is not the least suggestion—such as one may sometimes detect in the
earlier novels laid in Paris—of an artificial bringing together of characters and setting, of the scenery's being let down behind the figures.
It is one result of the method of James that his people seem to belong
in their setting. It has had time to grow up about them; they have had
time to take on the coloration of their environment. Chad and Maria
Gostrey and Little Bilham, as well as Gloriani and Madame de Vionnet, have quite the air of natives; and we are invited to behold the
entire process of acclimatization of Lambert Strether.

The characters are Paris spiritual. And as the physical atmosphere
is one of suffused and tempered light, so the spiritual atmosphere is
one of intelligence tempered with imagination. When Strether looks
back so wistfully on his earlier visit to Paris, when he regrets the subsequent employments which have cheated him of "life," it is the life
of the intelligence that he has in mind. He thinks of all the "movements" he has missed through his absence from the capital of the
world. He thinks of all the *talk,*—talk freely and genially ranging
without vulgar hindrance over the fields of life and art, which in such
a view are not to be divorced. He has done the best he could for himself in Woollett. He has attached himself to the woman of highest intelligence and most imposing character in the place. He has published
a magazine with a green cover. But he has not enjoyed there the intellectual amenities for which he has himself such an unusual aptitude.
He has never found intelligence tempered with imagination, intelligence made sociable. The errand that takes him abroad proves to be
his great occasion for making up arrears. The fortunate encounter
with Maria Gostrey opens his eyes to the possibilities of discriminating
thought on many subjects. Europe, on her showing, appears to be an
institution offering special facilities for play of mind and imagination.
The problem confronting him is not so bald and simple as he had
been led to believe. It is a subject calling for planned and gradual
stages of approach. It has as many aspects as a problem in metaphysics,
and must be considered again and again from one side and another. It
is a fortress of many circumvallations, or a Jericho that must be seven

times encircled before its walls will tumble to the blowing of his trumpet. He must not let himself be bullied or hurried into a decision by his own interest or by any moral prejudice or anxiety. He may allow himself—what is, we feel, the luxury he most craves—that clear impartiality of consideration which is so congenial to the Gallic spirit.

If there is one of his characters whom we are tempted to identify with Henry James himself, it is Lambert Strether. His rôle calls more than any other for this brooding exercise of a mind detached upon the human spectacle. His maturity and independence, his sympathetic and discriminating quality of mind, his patience and the unfailing satisfaction he takes in the interpretation of his subject, all make us think again and again of the author of these novels and the man who sat for Mr. Sargent's portrait. And in this story, so given shape by the intelligence of this character, James fashioned for himself the most perfect vehicle for his own habit of reflection. He is himself, like Strether, profoundly moral in his sentiment. But he and his creature both seem to feel that, if the intelligence is to be used for the eventual benefit of the moral passion, it must not be warped by any moral pressure; it must be left absolutely free to reach its own conclusions. And for both of them the greatest of pleasures is that extended rumination over life by which its true values may come to be appreciated. The tone of "The Ambassadors" is accordingly the nearest we ever come to the very tone of Henry James. It is the tone of large and sociable speculation upon human nature, a tone at once grave and easy, light and yet deep, earnest and yet free from anxiety. It is the tone, most of all, of the leisurely thinker, well-assured that maturity can be the product only of time. And what he offers us are fruits well ripened in the sun of his thought.

The Ambassadors

by F. O. Matthiessen

The Ambassadors, the first of James' three crowning works to be completed,[1] has proved by far his most popular book with the critics. In this they have followed his lead, since he announced in the preface that it was "frankly, quite the best, 'all round,' " of all his productions. He wrote it with gusto, declaring to Howells as he felt his way into its composition in the summer of 1900, that it was "human, dramatic, international, exquisitely 'pure,' exquisitely everything . . . My genius, I may even say, absolutely thrives." Such fresh confidence carried into the texture of the book. After the strained virtuosity of *The Awkward Age* and *The Sacred Fount,* James expanded into a theme that was both opulent and robust. He expressed the mood that had been phrased by Longfellow's brother-in-law Tom Appleton: "All good Americans, when they die, go to Paris." Appleton was talking of the era directly after the Civil War, the era James had recorded in *The American.* But the mood was to persist, and for the next post-war period, for the generation of the nineteen-twenties, Paris was still the same "huge iridescent" jewel it was for Strether, the symbol of liberation from every starved inadequate background into life.

"The Ambassadors" by *F. O. Matthiessen. From* Henry James: The Major Phase *(New York, 1944), pp. 18–23, 38–41. Copyright 1944 by Oxford University Press, Inc. Reprinted by permission of the publisher.

[1] *The Wings of the Dove* appeared in 1902, *The Ambassadors* not until 1903. But *The Ambassadors* had been finished by the summer of 1901, and this reversal of the order in which they were written was caused by its acceptance for serialization in *The North American Review* (January–December, 1903). One application that James had made of what he had learned through his plays of the art of the Scenario was in his long preliminary sketches or "projects" for both these novels. He referred to these sketches, in a letter to Wells (November, 1902), as being exceptional to his former practice, and said that the one for *The Ambassadors* ran to twenty thousand words, that for *The Wings* to only half such length. He added that he had destroyed the latter. The former he had submitted to Harper's as the basis for serialization, and believed to have been destroyed by them. But it was rescued from their files and published, in part, by Edna Kenton in the James number of *The Hound and Horn* (Spring, 1934). If there was a comparable scenario for *The Golden Bowl,* it presumably has also been destroyed.

What caused James' preference for the book was not its theme, but its roundness of structure. On the same grounds of " 'architectural' competence" his second favorite was *The Portrait of a Lady*. In *The Ambassadors* we have a fine instance of the experienced artist taking an external convention, and, instead of letting it act as a handicap, turning it to his own signal advantage. James had always been uneasy —as well he might have been—with his age's demand for serialized fiction. But here for once he felt a great stimulus to his ingenuity, and he laid out his novel organically in twelve books, each of which could serve for a month's installment. His subject was well fitted to such treatment, since it consisted in Strether's gradual initiation into a world of new values, and a series of small climaxes could therefore best articulate this hero's successive discoveries. It is interesting to note also the suspense that James creates by the device of the delayed intro-duction of the chief characters in Strether's drama.

The opening book at Chester, where Strether, arriving from Liver-pool to meet his friend Waymarsh, encounters first Maria Gostrey, is really a prologue that strikes the theme of Europe—the Europe of old houses and crooked streets which was also being stamped upon Ameri-can imaginations by James' contemporary, Whistler. The second book begins in London, and though Strether is already started on his eager growth through fresh impressions, how far he still has to go is indi-cated by Maria's remark that the theater which he takes "for—com-paratively—divine" is "impossible, if you really want to know." Dur-ing this conversation Chad Newsome's name is first casually introduced, and then followed by expertly swift exposition of the situation which Strether has come out to rectify. But we don't see Chad himself for some time yet. Strether must have his initial taste of Paris, that "vast bright Babylon." And as he stands in the Boulevard Malesherbes look-ing up at the balcony of Chad's apartment, he recognizes in a flash, in the essence of Jamesian revelation, that the life which goes on in such balanced and measured surroundings cannot possibly be the crude dis-sipation that Woollett, Massachusetts, believes. His initiation has reached its crucial stage.

Only at the end of this third book does Chad himself appear, with a dramatic entrance into the back of Maria's and Strether's box at the Comédie. In a neat instance of how he could meet the devices of the serial, James has him sit there through the darkness of the act, with Strether intensely conscious of his presence; and brings the two of them face to face in conversation not until after the play, at the beginning of book four. In that book Strether tactfully feels his way into friend-ship with Chad; and in the next he is introduced to Madame de Vion-net. It is significant that the declaration for life which was the seed of this novel flowers into its full form, as spoken by Strether to Little Bilham, immediately after this introduction. The next two books concentrate on Strether's developing relationship with Madame de Vionnet, from his first call on her to his boldly flouting Woollett and taking her out to lunch. Before the end of this book, a little more than half way through the novel, his position and Chad's are reversed: Chad says he is willing to go home and it is Strether who now urges him to stay.

Such conduct brings its swift retribution, with the arrival, in book eight, of the new ambassador, Mrs. Newsome's formidable daughter Sarah Pocock, who has been sent to take over the duties of the wavering Strether. The portrait of the Pococks—Sarah, Jim, and Mamie—is one of James' triumphs in light-handed satire, in the manner he had mastered in *Daisy Miller* and had developed further in that lesser known but delightful *jeu d'esprit, The Reverberator*. With the Pococks the cast is finally complete, and it is an astonishing tribute to James' skill that the most intensely realized presence in the novel is that of Mrs. Newsome, who never appears at all and yet looms massively like "some particularly large iceberg in a cool blue northern sea."

The critical point in book nine is the announcement that Madame de Vionnet's daughter is to be married, which leaves Strether, blind until now to the actual situation, with the growing awareness that it must be Madame de Vionnet herself to whom Chad is somehow bound. The tenth book moves rapidly to Sarah's being outraged at what she regards as Strether's treachery to her mother, and to her ultimatum that her entourage is leaving Paris. The eleventh book rises to the most effective climax of all, Strether's glimpse of Chad and Madame de Vionnet together on the river, and his long-delayed perception of their real relationship. What is left for the concluding book is his final interview with Madame de Vionnet, which James was inclined to regard as the novel's "most beautiful and interesting" scene. Then, after a last talk with Chad, Strether faces with Maria what the whole experience has come to mean for him.

What most concerned James in this structure was also his principal contribution to the art of the novel, his development in Strether of a center of consciousness. What Strether *sees* is the entire content, and James thus perfected a device both for framing and for interpreting experience. All art must give the effect of putting a frame around its subject, in the sense that it must select a significant design, and, by concentrating upon it, thus empower us to share in the essence without being distracted by irrelevant details. James' device serves greatly to reinforce such concentration, since if every detail must be observed and analysed by Strether, we obtain a heightened singleness of vision. We obtain both "the large unity" and "the grace of intensity" which James held to be the final criteria for a novel. His contribution here has been fully assessed by critics, and has been assimilated in varying degrees by many subsequent novelists. Indeed, some have gone so far as to declare *The Ambassadors* the most skillfully planned novel ever written. The chief reminder we need now is that there is a vast difference between James' method and that of the novels of "the stream of consciousness." That phrase was used by William James in his *Principles of Psychology*, but in his brother's novels there is none of the welling up of the darkly subconscious life that has characterized the novel since Freud. James' novels are strictly novels of intelligence rather than of full consciousness; and in commenting on the focus of attention that he had achieved through Strether, he warned against "the terrible *fluidity* of self-revelation."

* * *

But what does Strether finally make of his experience? The issue at the close shows how rigorously James believed that an author should hold to his structure. He had posited his hero's sense that it was too late for him to live; and had reinforced this with Strether's New England scrupulosity that in siding with Chad his conscience could be clear, since there was to be "nothing in it for himself." And no matter how bewilderingly iridescent he finds the jewel-image of Paris, since "what seemed all surface one moment seemed all depth the next," Strether never loses his moral sense. James seems to have taken his own special pleasure in avoiding the banal by not making Paris the usual scene of seduction but instead the center of an ethical drama. Another aspect of the structure—and its most artificial—is the rôle of *ficelle* conceived for Maria Gostrey. She exists only as a confidante for Strether, only as a means of letting him comment on his experience. Consequently, as James himself noted, she had a "false connexion" with the plot which he had to bend his ingenuity to make appear as a real one. But his device of having her fall in love with Strether and hope wistfully to marry him does not achieve such reality.

It serves rather to exaggerate the negative content of Strether's renunciation. He has come at last, as he says, to *see* Mrs. Newsome, and we know by now how much is involved in that word. But he leaves Paris and Maria to go back to no prospect of life at all. We are confronted here with what will strike us much more forcibly in *The Golden Bowl*, the contrast in James between imputed and actual values. The burden of *The Ambassadors* is that Strether has awakened to a wholly new sense of life. Yet he does nothing at all to fulfill that sense. Therefore, fond as James is of him, we cannot help feeling his relative emptiness. At times, even, as when James describes how "he went to Rouen with a little handbag and inordinately spent the night," it is forced upon us that, despite James' humorous awareness of the inadequacy of his hero's adventures, neither Strether nor his creator escape a certain soft fussiness.

What gives this novel the stamina to survive the dated flavor of Strether's liberation is the quality that James admired most in Turgenieff, the ability to endow some of his characters with such vitality that they seem to take the plot into their own hands, or rather, to continue to live beyond its exigencies. The center of that vitality here is the character not reckoned with in James' initial outline. For what pervades the final passages is Strether's unacknowledged love for Madame de Vionnet. James has succeeded in making her so attractive that, quite apart from the rigid requirement of his structure, there can really be no question of Strether's caring deeply for any other woman. The means that James used to evoke her whole way of life is a supreme instance of how he went about to give concrete embodiment to his values. Just as he devoted the greatest care to the surroundings for Strether's declaration and explicitly drew on his own memories of the garden behind the house where Madame Récamier had died, so he created Madame de Vionnet entirely in terms of and inseparable from old Paris. Every distinction in her manner is related to Strether's impression of her house, where each chair and cabinet suggests "some glory, some prosperity of the First Empire, some Napoleonic glamour, some dim lustre of the great legend." In his "summing up" James had attempted to convey why the great English houses had grown to mean so much to him. It was primarily their "accumulations of expression": "on the soil over which so much has passed, and out of which so much has come," they "rose before me like a series of visions . . . I thought of stories, of dramas, of all the life of the past—of things one can hardly speak of; speak of, I mean at the time. It is art that speaks of those things; and the idea makes me adore her more and more."

That gives us insight into why James, to a greater degree than any other American artist, was a spokesman for the imagination as a conserving force. He believed that art is the great conserver, since it alone can give permanence to the more perishable order of society. Yet, despite the usual view of him, James dwelt very little in the past. His impressions and his reading were preponderantly, almost oppressively, contemporary. His one living tap-root to the past was through his appreciation of such an exquisite product of tradition as Madame de Vionnet. Yet, as he created her, she was the very essence of the aesthetic sensibility of his own day. Strether can hardly find enough com-

parisons for her splendor. Her head is like that on "an old precious
medal of the Renaissance." She is "a goddess still partly engaged in a
morning cloud," or "a sea-nymph waist-high in the summer surge."
She is so "various and multifold" that he hardly needs to mention
Cleopatra. And though Mona Lisa is not mentioned, James is evoking
something very like Pater's spell. Although James' moral residues are
considerably different from Pater's, both Strether and James could
have subscribed to much of Pater's famous exhortation for fullness of
life, particularly to the sentence which urges that one's passion should
yield "this fruit of a quickened, multiplied consciousness."

But Madame de Vionnet is more human than Pater's evocation. On
the last night that Strether sees her, she seems older, "visibly less exempt from the touch of time." And though she is still "the finest and
subtlest creature" he has ever met, she is, even as Shakespeare's Cleopatra, troubled like "a maid servant crying for her young man." In an
image which enables him to fuse the qualities with which he especially
wants to endow her, James makes Strether think that her dress of "simplest coolest white" is so old fashioned "that Madame Roland must on
the scaffold have worn something like it." Madame de Vionnet's end
is also to be tragic. She has learned from life that no real happiness
comes from taking: "the only safe thing is to give." Such a nature is
far too good for Chad, and she realizes now that "the only certainty"
for the future is that she will be "the loser in the end." Her positive
suffering and loss are far more affecting than Strether's tenuous renunciation.

The Loose and Baggy Monsters
of Henry James

by Richard P. Blackmur

It is interesting to observe—and I think it can equally be observed of
most great European novels—that the Aristotelian terms recognition
and reversal of roles apply sharply to the major motions of the plot
and that complication or intrigue applies firmly to the minor motions.
But instead of the journey of *hubris* or overweening pride, we have
the journey of the pilgrim, the searcher, the finder. And instead of
katharsis—the purging in pity and terror—we follow rather the Christian pattern of re-birth, the fresh start, the change of life or heart—
arising from the pity and terror of human conditions met and seen—
with the end not in death but in the living analogue of death, sacrifice, and renunciation. So it is in James; and so it is in Tolstoy with
the difference that sacrifice may take the form of death as with Anna
in *Anna Karenina,* subsidence into the run of things as with Levin in
that book or with Pierre in *War and Peace,* or disappearance into the
heroic unknown as with Vronsky in *Anna Karenina.* In James the end
is always a heightened awareness amounting to an exemplary conscience for life itself, accomplished by the expense, the sacrifice, the
renunciation of life as lived in the very conditions on which the consciousness and the conscience are meant to prevail. James's novels
leave us with the terrible exemplars of conscience seen coping with
the worst excruciations of which their consciousnesses are capable. The
order in the three late novels is interesting, and it is the order of composition if not of publication. Strether, in *The Ambassadors,* is the
exemplar of the life of senses. Kate Croy, in *The Wings of the Dove,*
is our lady of philosophy or practical wisdom shown as the exemplar
of all that is torn and dismayed, but still persistent in that role. Mag-

gie Verver, in *The Golden Bowl,* is perhaps as near the exemplar as
James could come to our lady of theology or divine wisdom; she is
James's creation nearest to Dante's Beatrice, stern and full of charity,
the rock itself but all compassion, in the end knowing all but absorbing all she knows into her predetermined self, not exactly lovable but
herself. Not that James would have admitted any of these conceptions
except the first.

For in the first, which is Strether as the life of senses, that is exactly
what James's own language shows: Strether's consciousness and his
conscience are applied to render an indirect view of the beauty and the
excruciation of the life of the senses: he assents to it, he knows it, but
he is only an exemplar of knowledge and assent: he himself is not
finally up to that life. This James clearly must have meant.

*   *   *

In the havoc as it moves and shapes and heaves is the underlying
form of the book: the form in which is apprehended the conditions
of life. The strongest shape and the sharpest motion—the deepest
heaving qualm—James is able to create out of that havoc is the shap-
ing in heaving motion of a conscience out of consciousness. The structure and the gradual emergence of that conscience seem to me the
overt and visible acknowledgment of the underlying form. Conscience
is the bite of things known together, in remorse and in incentive; conscience is that unification of the sense of things which is moral beauty;
conscience comes at many moments but especially, in James, in those
deeply arrested moments when the will is united with the imagination
in withdrawal.

It is on such moments that each of our three novels ends. In *The
Golden Bowl* the Prince tells Maggie "I see nothing but you." That
means he is united with his conscience. "And the truth of it had with
this force after a moment so strangely lifted his eyes that as for pity
and dread of them she buried her own in his breast." The moment
was gone. At the end of *The Wings of the Dove* our lady of philosophy
Kate Croy and her lover Merton Densher feel stretch over them the
dove's wings of the dead Milly Theale. "She turned to the door, and
her headshake was now the end. 'We shall never again be as we were.' "
Beauty and a shade had passed between.

So it was too with Strether in *The Ambassadors* and there are
thoughts in his mind toward the end of that book, applied to the
wonderful mistress of the caddish young man he had come to Paris to
rescue, but fitting exactly the situation in other books as well. "It was
actually moreover as if he didn't think of her at all, as if he could
think of nothing but the passion, mature, abysmal, pitiful, she repre-

sented, and the possibilities she betrayed." These were the powers the image of moral beauty—of conscience—had attempted to transform. It is the perennial job of uprooted imagination, of conscience, choosing from beauty and knowledge, to raise such an image; but it may not transgress actuality without destruction; the images must not be mistaken for reality though the heart craves it. As Dante says (*Purg.* XXI–133–36):

> *Or puoi la quantitate*
> *comprender dell'amar ch'a te mi scalda,*
> *quando dismento nostra vanitate,*
> *trattando l'ombre come cosa salda*

Now may you comprehend the measure of the love that warms me toward you, when I forget our nothingness, and treat images as solid things.

The poor shade of the poet Statius had tried to embrace Vergil, and these were Vergil's words in answer. There the shadow was the only actual. It is interesting to use an insight from Dante here, because in his construction of conscience and moral beauty, James is himself making a late gesture in the aesthetic-moral tradition of the Christian world which Dante did so much to bring into poetry. With both men, it was only a hair's breadth, a mere change of phase, between the spiritual and the sensual, the ideal and the actual; and this is because there was in them both the overwhelming presence of felt, of aesthetic, reality as it fastened like a grapple upon individual souls and bodies.

Also to think of Dante here may remind us again of the great intellectual spiritual form in which James worked: the form of conversion, rebirth, the new life. That is the experience of Strether seen against the actual world, and in that world—"in the strict human order." Not a tragedy in the old sense—that is in its end—its tragedy lies in its center: in the conditions of life which no conversion, no rebirth, no turning, ever leaves behind—not even in saints till they have gone to heaven. The tragic tension lies partly between what is re-born and what is left over, and partly between the extremes toward which conversion always runs and the reality which contains the extremes.

The extremes with which Henry James was obsessed had largely to do with the personal human relations and almost nothing at all to do with public relations except as they conditioned, marred, or made private relations. It may be said that James wooed into being—by seeing what was there and then going on to create what might be there in consciousness and conscience—a whole territory of human relations hitherto untouched or unarticulated. I do not say not experienced, only unarticulated. So excessive is this reach into relation, there is no escape possible for the creatures caught in it except by a deepening or thickening of that relation until, since it cannot be kept up, it must be sacrificed. That is to say, its ideal force becomes so great that its mere actual shade becomes intolerable. So it was with Strether; he denied Marie de Vionnet and Maria Gostrey wholly in order to be 'right' with the ideal which the actual experience of them had elicited in his mind. But the denial was a gesture of this ideal, and it could have been otherwise, could in another soul have been the gesture of assent; for the beauty and the knowledge were still there, and the reality, which contains both the ideal and the actual, and so much more, stands, in its immensity, behind.

Behind is a good place. If we think of what is behind, and feel what we think, which is what James did, we will understand all the better the desperation out of which Strether created his image of moral beauty, the virtuous connection, and how it stood up, no matter what, as conscience. Otherwise, like Strether at his low point, we "mightn't see anyone any more at all." As it is we see with Maria Gostrey: "It isn't so much your *being* 'right'—it's your horrible sharp eye for what makes you so."

We have gotten, as we meant to, rather far away from the mere executive form—gotten into what that form merely articulates and joints and manipulates and takes into itself, itself being charged and modified thereby; but it has been there all along, that form, and we can now look at at least one facet of it with double vision: to see what it is and to see at the same time what happens to it—like what happens to a meter—in use. There are many possibilities—all those executive habits of the artist James names in his Prefaces, some of them never named before; and all those other devices, rhetorical and imagistic which James uses without naming—but for my purpose, which is to show how a technical device criticizes the substance it puts in motion and how the substance modifies the device, there is none so handy or so apt as James's use of the conventional figure of the confidante, a figure common to European drama, but developed to the highest degree of conventionality in the French theater James knew best.

Each of the three novels has examples, and in each the uses to which they are put are somewhat different. In the theater the confidante is used to let the audience know what it otherwise would not; she blurts out secrets; carries messages; cites facts; acts like a chorus; and is otherwise generally employed for comic relief or to represent the passage of time. Generally speaking, the confidante is stupid, or has the kind of brightness that goes with gossip, cunning, and malice. In these three novels the case is different: each confidante has a kind of bottom or residual human stupidity and each is everlastingly given to gossip; but the gossip has a creative purpose—to add substance to the story—and the stupidity is there to give slowness and weight and alternative forms to the perceptions and responses which they create. This is the gossiping stupidity for which there is no name in any living language, but which the Sanskrit calls *Moha,* the vital, fundamental stupidity of the human race by which it represents, to the human view, the cow, or as we would say the sheep. It is what the man has been caught in when he gives you a sheepish look; he was caught a little short of the possibility he was trying to cope with. It is this role—so much more fundamental than the conventional original—that James's confidante is given to play; and saying so much it should be evident that she will qualify as well as report action, she will give it substance, and gain substance by it, as well as precipitate it.

*   *   *

Maria Gostrey, in *The Ambassadors,* shares the gossip and the creativeness of the Assinghams, but with the difference that she is the go-between who has something in common with both things she goes between, and that her creativeness is not a substitute and seldom a mistake, for she is, rather, when she pushes herself, clairvoyant. That she pushes herself often makes her a part of the story and part of the emotion that holds the story together. The gift of clairvoyance, the gift of seeing so into the center of things as to become a part of them, and of doing so merely by nature and the skill of a lifetime, gives her powers quite opposite to those of the Assinghams. Instead of hopelessness she creates hope, instead of futility possible use, instead of emptiness fullness; and she never makes tolerable that which ought to remain intolerable. That is why she becomes, in the deep sense, a part of the story, and why the story lifts her from a means to a substance. If it were not that a device ought not to be called so, I would say that this instance of the conventional device of the confidante was also an instance of classic form.

There remains the middle ground of what is nowadays called the mind or the intellect to enquire into: the conceptual, dogmatic, tendentious part of the whole mind: the part inhabited and made frantic by one's ideology. Although there has been a good deal of talk to the effect that James was defective in this quarter, I think all that talk will vaporize on the instant if the question underlying the talk is differently put. Not what ideas did James have, but with what ideas—abroad then and now—is James's imaginative response to life related? It will be these ideas that will illuminate and partake of his underlying form. In short we want to get at the ideas in James's mind that were related to his whole work; and in James these occupy a precarious but precious place. He is not a Dante or a Thomas Mann; his humanism is under cover, part of his way of seeing, part of his "deep-breathing economy of organic form."

But it had got twisted by his time and by the superstitions of his time; for although he was 'against' his time he had necessarily to collaborate with it—from the very honesty of his inward eye for the actual, no one more so. I do not know that the nature of this collaboration can be made plain, but a few generalizations may be risked. They have to do with the tendency toward expressionism in art and social thinking, which stem from what is meant by art for art's sake, and they have to do with the emergence of a new concept of the individual as isolated and detached from society in everything but responsiveness, which is a concept that springs, I think, from those changes in society that are related to the facts of population growth and the mass-form of society.

There is a sense in which art for art's sake as we have had it since the *Parnassiens* is itself a reflection of the shift in the bases and the growth in size of any given modern society. As the bourgeois base turns into the industrial base—as the great population engulfs the 'great society'—we get on the one hand something called pure poetry with a set of feelings in the poets who write it which has something to do with the impulse to escape (to deny, to cut away) and the conviction of isolation (the condition of the incommunicable, the purely expressive, the fatally private—the sense of operating at a self-created parallel to the new society). At the same time, on the other hand, we get a belief in that monster the pure individual, whose impulse is to take life as a game, and whose ambition is to make the individual *feeling* of life the supreme heroism; so that the tropes of one's own mind become the only real parallel to life. In both cases—in pure art and in the pure individual—we pretend that it was like this in the past just behind our past.

No doubt this is so of some past, but not where it is looked for, in the Great Europe. It is more likely so in some of the over-populated periods in Egyptian or Byzantine history, or in the Rome of the second century: each of which ended in the culture of the fellaheen, where the individual was purified to extinction, from which only Rome has so far recovered. What we overlook in our pretense to a tradition is the difference between a population-burst accompanied by the disappearance of knowledge and the shrinking of the means of subsistence, which is what the past shows us (Egypt, China, India, Rome) and a great continuing population growth accompanied by the division of culture and the specialization of knowledge, along with the tremendous multiplication of the means of subsistence and of war—all of which has been our experience. What we see is the disappearance of the old establishment of culture—culture safe from the ravages of economy—and we do not know whether another culture is emerging from the massive dark, or, if it is, whether we like it. Whatever has disappeared or is emerging is doing so without loss of vitality except in the cultural establishment (now everywhere a prey to the economy) and with otherwise what seems a gain in vitality. What has above all survived in our new mass society is the sense of the pure individual— by himself, or herself, heir to all the ages. Because of the loss of the cultural establishment we have put a tremendous burden on the pure individual consciousness. It seems to us that in order to hang on to the pure individual we must burden his consciousness beyond any previous known measure. We make him in our art, especially the art of literature, assume the weight of the whole cultural establishment—above all that part of it which has to do with behavior, manners, human relations: with insight, with conformity and rebellion, and with the creation or ability to create absorbing human motives. For all this the artist has to find, by instinct since his culture does not sufficiently help him, what I called to begin with the underlying classic form in which things are held together in a living way, with the sense of life going on.

Sometimes this burden of consciousness seems to obscure, if not to replace, the individuals we create, whether in ourselves or in our arts. At any rate, this burden of consciousness is what has happened to our culture. There is no longer any establishment, no longer any formula, and we like to say only vestigial forms, to call on outside ourselves. There is only the succession of created consciousnesses—each of which is an attempt to incorporate, to give body to, to incarnate so much as it is possible to experience, to feel it, the life of the times, including the culture no matter what has happened to it—and including also of course all those other things which never were in any culture, but which press on us just the same.

These generalizations seem to me one of the useful backgrounds against which to look at the novels of Henry James. As background it reflects light on the extremes to which he pushed the limits of his created individual consciousnesses, so much less varied than those of Gide, Proust, Mann, Kafka, and Joyce, but no less intense, no less desperately grasping after life, and the form of life, for and in the name of the individual. In that light we can but understand what Strether, in *The Ambassadors,* is up to when he says *Live all you can!* We can understand also how Mme. de Vionnet, the young man's splendid mistress, is up to the same thing under what are fundamentally the same conditions. We understand how much there is to see—to see unaided by ourselves—how much there is to intensify into form—in the simplest relation between human beings.

James at fifty-eight, when he wrote *The Ambassadors*, had experienced and therefore could dramatize the disestablishment of culture and the shift in the bases of society, and he could do so all the better because he did not, and probably could not, have understood them intellectually or historically. He was concerned with the actuality he found and with the forms under the actuality. He was himself an example of disestablishment and a forerunner of what we may expect to find a prevalent form of disinherited sensibility, the new 'intellectual proletariat,' and he had therefore only to write out of himself against the society which 'intellectually' or by common assumption he thought still existed, in order to create an extreme type of transitional image of the future time. Not unnaturally his original audience—barring the young who were ahead of themselves—thought he had created sterile fantasies; the richer his subjects grew and the deeper he got into them, the more his sales fell off. His own experience of 'America' and of 'Europe,' where America had apparently moved faster than Europe toward the mass society, toward the disinheritance but not the disappearance of the individual, had moved him ahead of his contemporaries; had moved him to the 1930's when he began to be read seriously, and the '40's when he got to be the rage, and now to the '50's when he seems, so to speak, an exaggerated and highly sensitized form of the commonplace of our experience: the sensitized deep form.

If Strether is our example of 1902 looking ahead, what Strether would feel now would seem like the music of Adrian Leverkühn in Mann's *Doctor Faustus*: a heightening but not a disintegration of his feelings of 1902; and it would be a heightening, as in Mann's novel, by parody and critique, because like Leverkühn he would have had so much more of the same thing behind him, and so much more of the same burden put upon him, than he had in the earlier time. Our theoretic new Strether would have found out how much more had to be re-established in a form greater than its own than he had then felt; how much more, by necessity and by choice, must be reborn into actuality out of its hidden form. But the difference between the two Strethers would be by bulk and by kind, not by quality, by scope and not by reach. The reach is into the dark places where the Muses are, and all the rest is the work we do to bring into the performance of our own language the underlying classic form in which they speak.

The Art of Henry James: *The Ambassadors*

by Joan Bennett

The Ambassadors is a novel not a treatise and not (as one modern critic has suggested) an allegory. In allegory the idea precedes and governs the fable; what James thought of this form is made clear in his book about Hawthorne where he writes:

> Hawthorne, in his metaphysical moods, is nothing if not allegorical, and allegory, to my sense, is quite one of the lighter exercises of the imagination . . . I frankly confess that I have as a general thing but little enjoyment of it and that it has never seemed to me a first rate literary form. . . . It is apt to spoil two good things—a story and a moral—a form and a meaning.

In *The Ambassadors* both are unspoiled; the moral content depends on a series of impressions arrived at because of what happens and the way in which happenings are presented. We experience the content of this novel through the consciousness of Strether. He is not always present; he does not narrate the story; he is, however, present at every important scene (it is important because of its effect on him), and no character in the novel is better known to us than to him; we know them only as he knows them and because he knows them. But the "only" need not disturb us. When James decided that all the experience of the book should come to the reader through Strether he knew that Strether must be a man of perception—one capable of learning from experience. To see a character or a place as Strether sees them is to see them with penetration. As to the disposition and proportioning of the story it will perhaps be enough to say that the exposition is not (as it sometimes is with James) too long. (By the end of the second book—there are twelve in all—we have all the data in our hands without having noticed any arrest in the action.) Every scene in the novel is relevant to Strether's central experience—his revaluation of all his values; everything leads up to and then on from

---

"The Art of Henry James: The Ambassadors*"* by *Joan Bennett. From the* Chicago Review, *IX* (*Winter, 1956*), *16–26. Reprinted by permission of the* Chicago Review.

the conversation with little Bilham in which the original germ of the
story unfolds itself in the speech containing the words "Live all you
can, it's a mistake not to."

The word "life" is, naturally, a key word in this novel; and the main
theme can be spot-lighted by isolating a number of points in the action
where Strether considers and reconsiders the content of that word.
It is worth while to look at four places in the novel where this happens.
The first scene I shall quote from occurs at the end of the exposition,
in the opening section of Book II. Strether is talking to Miss Gostrey
(who is his confidante throughout) and explaining what he has come
to Europe for. He tells her that if Chad goes home he will "come in for
a particular chance—a chance that any properly constituted young
man would jump at." An opening awaits him. It carries with it a large
share of the profits of the expanding business, but it of course requires
Chad's presence at Woollett.

> "That's what I mean by his chance. . . . And to see that he doesn't
> miss it is, in a word, what I've come out for."
> She let it all sink in. "What you've come out for then is simply to
> render him an immense service."
> Well, poor Strether was willing to take it so.
> "Ah, if you like."
> "He stands, as they say, if you succeed with him to gain—"
> "Oh a lot of advantages." Strether had them clearly at his fingers' ends.
> "By which you mean of course a lot of money."
> "Well, not only. I'm acting with a sense for him of other things too.
> Consideration and comfort and security—the general safety of being
> anchored by a strong chain. He wants, as I see him, to be protected.
> Protected, I mean, from life."

Miss Gostrey is quick to interpret this; evidently it is intended that
Chad will marry as well as becoming a successful business man. Later
in the novel we meet the intended young woman. But I want to arrest
that scene on the important sentence "Protected, I mean, from life."
From that let us turn to a scene from the second section of Book IV.
Strether has met Chad and received his shock of surprise. Instead of
finding the Chad he knew at Woollett or that same boy spoiled by a
life of dissolute idleness in Paris, he has found him improved out of
all recognition. Miss Gostrey has also been introduced to Chad.

> His [i.e., Strether's] impression of Miss Gostrey after her introduction
> to Chad was meanwhile an impression of a person almost unnaturally
> on her guard. He struck himself as at first unable to extract from her
> what he wished; though indeed *of* what he wished at this special junc-
> ture he would doubtless have contrived to make but a crude statement.
> It sifted and settled nothing to put to her, *tout bêtement*, as she often
> said, "Do you like him, eh?"—thanks to his feeling it actually the least

of his needs to heap up the evidence in the young man's favour. He repeatedly knocked at her door to let her have it afresh that Chad's case—whatever else of minor interest it might yield—was first and foremost a miracle almost monstrous. It was the alteration of the entire man and was so signal an instance that nothing else, for the intelligent observer could—could it?—signify. "It's a plot!" he declared—"There's more in it than meets the eye," he gave rein to his fancy. "It's a plant." His fancy seemed to please her. "Whose then?"

"Well, the party responsible is, I suppose, the fate that waits for one, the dark doom that rides. What I mean is that with such elements one can't count. I've but my poor individual, my modest human means. It isn't playing the game to turn on the uncanny. All one's energy goes to facing it, to tracking it. One wants, confound it, don't you see?" he confessed with a queer face—"One wants to enjoy anything so rare. Call it then life"—he puzzled it out—"call it poor dear old life, simply, that springs the surprise. Nothing alters the fact that the surprise is paralyzing, or at any rate engrossing—all, practically, hang it, that one sees, that one can see."

Strether's speech is humorous; it is fanciful; nevertheless it is serious; he has advanced a long way since the time when he could think of "life" simply as something against which Chad must be protected. Life is now inscrutable, uncanny—it is something one may enjoy, it can spring an engrossing surprise. Strether still hopes and believes that Chad will go home with him: his judgement of what is right is not yet changed; but what he most wants is to see more of Chad and to find out how the change in him has been brought about. It is in Section II of Book V that Strether gives his lecture on life to Chad's friend, little Bilham. Again the tone of his talk is not solemn, though it makes the young man momentarily so—"A contradiction," James comments, "of the innocent gaiety the speaker had wished to promote." Yet it represents the serious reflections that have occurred to Strether during the action. He no longer thinks of life either as something to be protected against or as merely something to be observed:

"Live all you can; it's a mistake not to. It doesn't so much matter what you do in particular, so long as you have your life. If you haven't had that what *have* you had? This place and these impressions—mild as you find them to wind a man up so; all my impressions of Chad and of people I've seen at *his* place—well, have had their abundant message for me, have just dropped *that* into my head."

By this time Strether has shed the Woollett view of life (he had told Miss Gostrey at their first meeting "Woollett isn't sure it ought to enjoy") but he has still much left to discover about "life."

I will quote from only one more scene in which the word "life" prominently figures. This is the last scene in the novel and Strether

is saying goodbye to Miss Gostrey. We know already that he has re-
nounced the possibility of remaining in Paris and of marrying this
good friend of his. I quote only an image that occurs to Strether as
he sits waiting for Miss Gostrey "in the cool shade of her little Dutch-
looking dining room,"

> To sit there was, as he had told his hostess before, to see life re-
> flected for the time in ideally kept pewter, which was somehow
> becoming, improving to life, so that one's eyes were held and comforted.

But life can only "for the time" be so reflected. Its actual complexity
and the difficult choices it offers is what, in the course of the action,
Strether has learnt to appreciate.

When we isolate these four scenes which represent Strether's gradual
discovery of new meanings in the word "life," we are following the
main structure of the novel. What these scenes indicate is that aspect
of the "buried bone" or "figure in the carpet" which James foresaw
could be unfolded from the originating anecdote. Something more
complex, rising up into the artist's consciousness only as he con-
templated and explored his theme, reveals itself often in his imagery.
Here for example is the description of Miss Gostrey's room as Strether
first sees it (not the little Dutch-looking dining room but her sitting
room):

> Her compact and crowded little chambers, almost dusky, as they at
> first struck him, with accumulations, represented a supreme general
> adjustment to opportunities and conditions. Wherever he looked he saw
> an old ivory or an old brocade, and he scarce knew where to sit for
> fear of a misappliance. The life of the occupant struck him of a sudden
> as more charged with possession even than Chad's or Miss Barrace's;
> wide as his glimpse had lately become of the empire of "things," what
> was before him still enlarged it; the lust of the eyes and the pride of
> life had indeed thus their temple. It was the innermost nook of the
> shrine—as brown as a pirate's cave. In the brownness were glints of gold;
> patches of purple were in the gloom; objects all that caught, through
> the muslin, with their high rarity, the light of the low windows. Nothing
> was clear about them but that they were precious, and they brushed his
> ignorance with their contempt as a flower, in a liberty taken with him,
> might have been whisked under his nose.

From the language and imagery of that description much of
Strether's response to his environment emerges. We are aware of his
sense of bewilderment—the puritan conscience wincing at the pagan
richness of Miss Gostrey's taste and also recognizing the predatoriness
that such treasure-hunting represents. He is impressed but also dismayed. He is intimidated but also critical. This "supreme general ad-

justment to opportunities and conditions" is associated with burdens
—she is "charged with possessions" and her possessions dominate her;
he has been noticing the "empire of *things*"—they represent that surrender to the world against which the Bible warns us. "The lust of the
eyes and the pride of life had indeed thus their temple." Worship and
piracy are brought together in his mind. "It was the innermost nook of
the shrine—as brown as a pirate's cave." When, at the end of the
book, he renounces the happiness Miss Gostrey offers and returns to
the life of Woollett, about which he now has no illusions, it is, among
other things, this "lust of the eyes and pride of life" he is renouncing.
Also he has seen and seen clearly another kind of empire. His impression of Mme de Vionnet's room is related to the impression of
Miss Gostrey's. In Mme de Vionnet's room he reflects that:

> He had never before, to his knowledge, had present to him relics, of
> any special dignity, of a private order—little old miniatures, medallions,
> pictures, books; books in leather bindings, pinkish and greenish, with
> gilt garlands on the back, ranged, together with other promiscuous
> properties, under the glass of brass-mounted cabinets. His attention
> took them all tenderly into account. They were among the matters that
> marked Mme de Vionnet's apartment as something quite different from
> Miss Gostrey's little museum of bargains and from Chad's lovely home;
> he recognized it as founded much more on old accumulations that had
> possibly from time to time shrunken than on any contemporary method
> of acquisition or form of curiosity. Chad and Miss Gostrey had rum-
> maged and purchased and picked up and exchanged, sifting, selecting,
> comparing, whereas the mistress of the scene before him, beautifully
> passive under the spell of transmission—transmission from her father's
> line he quite made up his mind—had only received, accepted and been
> quiet. When she hadn't been quiet she had been moved at the most to
> some occult charity to some fallen fortune. There had been objects she
> or her predecessors might even conceivably have parted with under
> need, but Strether couldn't suspect them of having sold old pieces to
> get "better" ones. They would have felt no difference as to better or
> worse. He could but imagine their having felt—perhaps in emigration,
> in proscription, for his sketch was slight and confused—the pressure of
> want or the obligation of sacrifice.

Thus Strether sees Mme de Vionnet "passive under the spell of trans-
mission." She is the inheritor of tradition and all that she does and is
—including her relation to Chad and the marriage she arranges for
her lovely, virginal, convent-bred daughter, belongs to the tradition of
Catholic, aristocratic France. Strether fully responds to the beauty of
that order as she represents it. Perhaps he responds also to Mme de
Vionnet's world with a sense that it is doomed. The scene from which
I have quoted occurs in the first half of the novel when Strether first

visits Mme de Vionnet's room. It is on another visit, nearly at the end
of the novel, that Strether seems to become aware of a menace surrounding his hostess' gracious way of living:

> The windows were all open, their redundant hangings swaying a
> little, and he heard once more, from the empty court, the small plash of
> the fountain. From beyond this, and as from a great distance—beyond
> the court, beyond the *corps de logis* forming the front—came, as if
> excited and exciting, the vague voice of Paris. Strether had all along
> been subject to sudden gusts of fancy in connection with such matters
> as these—odd starts of the historic sense, suppositions and divinations
> with no warrant but their intensity. Thus and so, on the eve of the
> great recorded dates, the days and nights of revolution, the sounds had
> come in, the omens, the beginnings broken out. They were the smell
> of revolution, the smell of the public temper—or perhaps simply the
> smell of blood.
>
> It was at present queer beyond words, "subtle" he would have risked
> saying, that such suggestions should keep crossing the scene; but it was
> doubtless the effect of thunder in the air, which had hung about all day
> without release. His hostess was dressed as for thunderous times, and
> it fell in with the kind of imagination we have just attributed to him
> that she should be in the simplest, coolest white, of a character so old-
> fashioned, if he were not mistaken, that Madame Roland must on the
> scaffold have worn something like it. This effect was enhanced by a
> small black fichu or scarf, of crêpe or gauze, disposed quaintly round
> her bosom and now completing as by a mystic touch the pathetic, the
> noble analogy.

It is perhaps in such a passage as this, with its memory of the
revolution and its hint of a threatened social order, as also in the
pirate imagery of the passage describing Miss Gostrey's room, that
Mr. Spender detected an "indictment of society as fierce as that of
Baudelaire, or indeed of a class-conscious Marxist." But here it is wise
to tread warily. Primarily James's intention in the two passages is to
contrast (through Strether's awareness) the acquisitiveness of the
American emigré with the passiveness of the aristocrat who has inherited historic possessions. Moreover, when he associates Mme de
Vionnet with a particular victim of the guillotine, he does not choose
an aristocrat but that Jacobin heroine, Mme Roland. What he thereby
suggests is not so much that Mme de Vionnet represents a threatened
social order as that she represents romantic courage and loyalty. She
is a victim prepared for sacrifice. The passage is the prelude to a
scene in which he discovers the full extent of her love for Chad and
of her foresight that she will lose him. She tells him at the close:
"There's not a grain of certainty in my future—for the only certainty

is that I shall be the loser in the end." There is a danger (as there always is when a critic isolates imagery from the context) that he may mistake the overtones for the tune. The novel treats of a number of human beings in a particular situation. Through his intimate contact with them and his gradual discovery of the quality of each individual and all the bearings of their predicament, Strether grows in wisdom and understanding—not of society (except indirectly)—but of the individuals who compose it. It is his sense of moral values that changes, and the novel is not concerned with any political or economic theories.

It is, I think, possible, in connection with another scene in which Mme de Vionnet figures, both to illustrate further how James associates her in our minds with historic heroism and romance, and at the same time to encounter Mr. Grahame Greene's opinion that James was "fascinated, repelled and absorbent" of the Roman Catholic church. At the beginning of the seventh book Strether wanders into *Notre Dame* driven by an impulse:

> . . . the impulse to let things be, to give them time to justify themselves or at least to pass. He was aware of having no errand in such a place but the desire not to be, for the hour, in certain other places; a sense of safety, of simplification, which each time he yielded to it he amused himself by thinking of as a private concession to cowardice. The great Church had no altar for his worship, no direct voice for his soul; but it was none the less soothing even to sanctity; for he could feel there what he couldn't elsewhere, that he was a plain man taking the holiday he had earned.

Throughout the scene Strether is aware of himself as escaping, temporarily, from the burden of human responsibilities; and he connects such an escape with cowardice. He can understand

> . . . how, within the precinct, for the real refugee, the things of the world could fall into abeyance. That was the cowardice, probably,—to dodge them, to beg the question, not to deal with it in the hard outer light; but his own oblivions were too brief, too vain, to hurt any one but himself, and he had a vague and fanciful kindness for certain persons whom he met, figures of mystery and anxiety, and whom, with observation for his pastime, he ranked as those who were fleeing from justice. Justice was outside, in the hard light, and injustice too; but one was as absent as the other from the air of the long aisles and the brightness of the many altars.

This does not seem to me the language of one who is "fascinated and repelled" (and I think it is fair to identify Strether with his author to the extent of guessing that in this they are at one.) It is the language

of secure detachment, such enough of his own position to contemplate
that of the believers with "a vague and fanciful kindness." Among those
who have interested him is one in particular,

> a lady whose supreme stillness, in the shade of one of the chapels, he
> had two or three times noticed. . . . She was not prostrate—not in any
> degree bowed, but she was strangely fixed, and her prolonged immobil-
> ity showed her, while he passed and paused, as wholly given up to the
> need, whatever it was, that had brought her there. She only sat and
> gazed before her, as he himself often sat; but she had placed herself,
> as he never did, within the focus of the shrine, and she had lost herself,
> he could easily see, as he would only have liked to do. She was not a
> wandering alien, keeping back more than she gave, but one of the
> familiar, the intimate, the fortunate, for whom these dealings had a
> method and a meaning. She reminded our friend—since it was the way
> of nine tenths of his current impressions to act as recalls of things
> imagined—of some fine, firm, concentrated heroine of an old story,
> something he had heard, read, something that, had he had a hand for
> drama, he might himself have written, renewing her courage, renewing
> her clearness, in splendidly protected meditation.

She proves, of course, to be Mme de Vionnet, and Mme de Vionnet is
a faithful child of the Roman Catholic Church. She is also a sinner,
since she is a married woman enjoying intimate relations with one who
is not her husband. She is clear-sighted and courageously aware of the
peril of her immortal soul. All this James's are communicates to us
through his story and by means of his imagery. But I detect nothing in
the presentation either of nostalgia for Roman Catholicism or of in-
dignation against it, any more than I can detect a message about a
doomed social order. In short, the novel seems to me to be about a
particular human situation—though one sufficiently serious and sufficiently deeply explored, sufficiently amusing and ironical too, to be
representative of universal human predicaments. The novel is not, in
my opinion, concerned with either politics or religion except in so far
as the selected human beings are molded by religious faiths and by
economic and social conditions.

I must differ also from another distinguished critic and attempt to
formulate an answer to him. Dr. Leavis writes of *The Ambassadors*
in his book *The Great Tradition:*

> What, we ask, is this, symbolized by Paris, that Strether feels himself
> to have missed in his own life? Has James himself sufficiently inquired?
> Is it anything adequately realized? If we are to take the elaboration of
> the theme in the spirit in which we are meant to take it, haven't we to
> take the symbol too much at the glamorous face value it has for Strether?
> Isn't, that is, the energy of the "doing" (and the energy demanded for

the reading) disproportionate to the issues—to any issues that are concretely held and presented?

It is characteristic of Leavis that he goes straight to the heart of the matter. Certainly these questions are the ones we should ask ourselves. The only adequate answers are contained in the novel itself—the work of art in which James unearths his buried bone. But some reader may be deterred from looking there by Leavis' implication that he will find nothing worth while. In case that should happen I will attempt to counterattack.

During the seven years that intervened between his hearing the anecdote and his writing *The Ambassadors* James was asking himself what it was "symbolized by Paris" that Strether felt himself to have missed. The answer is in the whole series of impressions we are made to share with him through the novel. Little more can be said, in other terms than James's own, except that he had missed those spontaneous joys that come from the contemplation of beauty, the culture of the mind and uncalculating love for a fellow-creature. It does not seem to James—and it does not seem to a reader who responds to his novel—that Paris has, by the end, a "glamorous face value" for Strether. It had something like that at the beginning of the book. But the Paris he renounces for himself contains cruelty, greed, and suffering as well as generosity, courage, and joy. The issues "concretely held and presented" are not, to my mind, disproportionate to the labor of writing or of reading because they are ever-relevant issues between true and false human values. Finally I should like to add that the "energy demanded for reading" is rewarded at every turn, not only because we share with James the discovery of important truths; but because we are continuously spell-bound by his story and amused by his irony, his wit, and his charm in presenting what he sees.

James The Old Intruder

by John E. Tilford, Jr.

The Ambassadors has long been acclaimed the Master's supreme example of the single point of view—"of employing but one centre," as he puts it, "and keeping it all within my hero's compass." Strether's consciousness was to be projected upon his "intimate adventure . . . from beginning to end without intermission or deviation," and it was "Strether's sense" of all other characters, "and Strether's only," that was to be shown.[1]

Admirers of James have borne ardent witness to the glorious fulfilment of this intention. Foremost is Percy Lubbock, in his widely esteemed *Craft of Fiction* (New York, 1921). Lubbock particularly emphasizes James's withdrawal, his standing aside, "to let Strether's thought tell its own story." The novel thus "never passes outside the circle of his thought": the subject covers "Strether's field of vision and [is] bounded by its limits; it consists entirely of an impression received by a certain man." Everything

> is represented from his point of view. To see it, even for a moment, from some different angle—if, for example, the author interposed with a vision of his own—would patently disturb the right impression. The author does no such thing, it need hardly be said. . . . There is no drawing upon extraneous sources of information; Henry James knows all there is to know of Strether, but he most carefully refrains from using his knowledge. He wishes us to accept nothing from him, on authority. . . .

James's "own part in the narration is now unobtrusive to the last degree. . . . His part in the effect is no more than that of the playwright, who vanishes and leaves his people to act the story. . . ." Hence, "Everything . . . is dramatically rendered . . . , because . . . no-

---

"James The Old Intruder," by John E. Tilford, Jr. From Modern Fiction Studies, *IV (Summer, 1958), 157–64. Reprinted by permission of* Modern Fiction Studies. *Copyright © 1958 by Purdue Research Foundation, Lafayette, Indiana.*

[1] Preface to *The Ambassadors*, in *The Art of the Novel: Critical Prefaces*, Introd. Richard P. Blackmur (New York, 1934), p. 317.

body is addressing us, nobody is reporting his impression to the reader.
. . . the book is all pictorial, an indirect impression received through
Strether's intervening consciousness, beyond which the story never
strays" (158–70).

Other critics have likewise believed. Martin W. Sampson states
that "literally everything that is to be presented" is from Strether's
point of view: "it is through him and through him only that the case
has come into our experience. . . ." R. P. Blackmur speaks of "the
considerations which led [James] to employ only one centre and to
keep it entirely in Strether's consciousness," to have the "adventure
. . . seen only through his eyes." Bruce McCullough claims that
James "went further than merely to refrain from intruding in the
manner of the confiding, commenting, moralizing author," but "man-
aged . . . even to eliminate himself to a considerable degree as an
impersonal narrator, or to conceal himself as such." The story "does
not appear to come either from James or from Strether. Nobody *tells*
it. It is not a report about something but the thing itself, enacted before our eyes." Joseph Warren Beach, more moderately, observes that
"James is seldom or never, in his later work [like *The Ambassadors*],
the 'omniscient author.' He has a great scorn for this slovenly way of
telling a story." He never absolutely carried out the "great concern"
of his later novels, "to maintain a beautiful consistency of point of
view," though he did carry the "principle . . . farther than any
writer had ever done." In *The Ambassadors* "the story is told from
beginning to end (except for slight variations in the first chapter) from
the point of view of the same person. . . . the extreme limit of the
dramatic tendency so far as this device is concerned," at least in 1903.[2]

An examination of the text itself, however, indicates that the centre
is by no means always kept within the "hero's compass" and that often
the novel does pass "outside the circle of his thought." Quite frequently the author interposes "with a vision of his own," and he has
not, like a playwright, vanished altogether. And the authorial intrusions are certainly not restricted to the first chapter, but continue
throughout the novel. One of James's obvious intrusions, for instance,
is the naming of his "centre." Many times he refers to his protagonist,
with kindly archness, as "poor Strether" (e.g., on 4, 14, 57, 61, 66, 172,
397), "poor man" (10), and at least once as "our hero" (88). More

---

[2] Sampson, Introd. to *The Ambassadors*, Harper's Modern Classics (New York,
1930), pp. vii–viii (all references are to this edition); Blackmur, Introd., *The Art
of the Novel*, p. xxxv; McCullough, *Representative English Novelists: Defoe to
Conrad* (New York, 1946), pp. 288–90; Beach, *The Method of Henry James* (Philadelphia, 1954; a reissue of the 1918 ed.), p. 56, and *The Twentieth Century Novel*
(New York, 1932), pp. 190, 197–98, 204.

noticeable is his frequent designation of Strether as "our friend," sometimes twice on a page (e.g., 20, 62, 119, 257). This phrase occurs more
than sixty-five times; familiar in nineteenth-century fiction, it inevitably implies an amiable understanding between the candid narrator and his gentle reader.

More significant is James's frequent appearance as the editorially
omniscient author, speaking frankly in the first person, taking his
reader into his confidence about his characters and about his own
part in telling the story. On the opening page he writes: "The principle I have just mentioned . . ." (3); and later he speaks of Strether's
prolonging "the meditation I describe" (62). Again and again one
notes such phrases as "incidents with which we have yet to make
acquaintance" (119), "as we know" (157), "as I have called it" (233),
"briefer than our glance at the picture" (272), "if we might so far dis-
criminate" (305), and "we have just seen" (417).

Sometimes James is almost as affably omniscient as Thackeray, however slovenly it might be. In addition to using innocuous constructions
like "it may be communicated" (8) and "It will have been sufficiently
seen" (62), he implicitly discusses with the reader his tribulations in
making the story: "All sorts of other pleasant small things . . . flowered in the air of the occasion; but the bearing of the occasion itself on
matters still remote concerns us too closely to permit us to multiply our
illustrations. Two or three, however, in truth, we should perhaps regret to lose" (11); "All sorts of things in fact now seemed to come over
him, comparatively few of which his chronicler can hope for space to
mention" (37); "If we should go into all that occupied our friend . . .
we should have to mend our pen" (96); and "he gave her the view,
vivid with a hundred more touches than we can reproduce, of what
had happened" (353). Occasionally James's intimate chat with his
reader almost makes us think (except for the style) that we have un-
wittingly strayed into George Eliot: "Only, his theory, as we know, had
bountifully been that the facts were, specifically, none of his business
. . . ; and since we have spoken of what he was, after his return, to recall and interpret, it may as well immediately be said that his real experience of these few hours put on . . . the aspect that is most to our
purpose" (386).

The last quotation also illustrates one of James's favorite methods
of interposing "with a vision of his own": that is, using "his knowledge"
to inform the reader of the future. Strether spends a morning with
Maria Gostrey "in a way that he was to remember, later on . . ." (27).
When Miss Gostrey tries to make Strether name the article produced
by Chad's manufactory, James slyly tells us: "But it may even now
frankly be mentioned that he, in the sequel, never *was* to tell her" (43).

Once, when Strether is puzzled, James says, "This was the very beginning with him of a condition as to which, later on, as will be seen, he found cause to pull himself up . . ." (80). Again, Strether spends an hour waiting for Chad—"one of those that he was to recall, at the end of his adventure, as the particular handful that most had counted" (362). And, for a final instance of this kind of intrusive omniscience, we find James saying:

> Why . . . the situation should have been really stiff, was . . . , so far as we are concerned, a question tackled, later on and in private, only by Strether himself. He was to reflect later . . . that it was mainly *he* who had explained . . . . Strether was to remember afterwards, further . . . ; and indeed he was to remember further still . . . (384–85; see also 93, 102, 156, 266).

This is hardly "the playwright, who vanishes and leaves his people to act the story."

James likewise makes liberal use of other routine privileges of the omniscient author. The first chapter, where, as Beach has observed, there are "slight variations" from the ideal, affords easy examples, as in the standard third-person description of Strether, actually from Miss Gostrey's point of view: "what his hostess saw, what she might have taken in with a vision kindly adjusted, was the lean, slightly loose figure of a man," and so on for a dozen lines (6). Sometimes James stands back a little from the scene, editorially commenting: "She was, however, like himself, marked and wan; only it naturally couldn't have been known to him how much a spectator looking from one to the other might have discerned that they had in common. . . . it made an apposition between them which he might well have shrunk from submitting to if he had fully suspected it" (8). Such interpositions —by no means limited to the first chapter—often exhibit a kind of tiptoe technique, in which James patters quietly back and forth between authorial omniscience and Strether's point of view. Early in Chapter II, for a typical specimen, we see Waymarsh as he appears to Strether; then follows a description, by no means filtered through Strether's consciousness, but frankly stated by author James:

> He had a large, handsome head, and a large, sallow, seamed face— a striking, significant physiognomic total, the upper range of which, the great political brow, the thick, loose hair, the dark, fuliginous eyes, recalled even to a generation whose standard had dreadfully deviated the impressive image, familiar by engravings and busts, of some great national worthy of the earlier part of the mid-century.

After a dozen more lines of such description, James stealthily shifts back to his "centre": "Strether, who had not seen him for a long interval, apprehended him now with a freshness of taste. . . ." The following sentences continue this shifting back and forth—as in this one, which opens with James omnisciently stating that "for some five years" they had not met, but before the sentence ends, he tiptoes back to Strether: "a fact that was in some degree an explanation of the sharpness with which, for Strether, most of his friend's features stood out." Another sentence begins omnisciently, then eases back to Strether: "Married at thirty, Waymarsh had not lived with his wife for fifteen years, and it came up vividly between them . . . that Strether was not to ask about her" (18–20). Many similar shifts may be found passim in the novel, notably when Strether and Miss Gostrey visit the theater (37), when he calls for his mail in Paris (53–55), and when he makes his acquaintance with Little Bilham (87).

The most extensive shifts of this kind occur in the two places James himself points out as "exquisite treacheries" to his method (Preface, 325–26)—his "hero's first encounter with Chad" (93f.) and Mamie Pocock's "single hour of suspense in the hotel salon" (301f.). To James, however, the "treacheries" are not shifting points of view but rather his substitution of the "representational effect" for the scenic method of presentation. He presumably does not recognize his frequent lapses not only from Strether's point of view but from objective narration as well. In the first of these "representations" James stands off, looks at his people, and freely shifts to and from Strether's consciousness. He is at first neutrally omniscient: "They couldn't talk without disturbing the spectators . . . ; and it . . . came to Strether . . . that these were the accidents of a high civilization. . . ." Then he passes outside the circle of Strether's thought and comments on our friend's discomfiture: "A reflection a candid critic might have made of old, for instance, was that it would have been happier for the son to look more like the mother; this was a reflection that at present would never occur" (96). In addition, he predicts the future (93, 95, 96) and discusses with his reader how much he should go into "all that occupied our friend" (96). In the chapter concerned with Mamie, the same kinds of shifts occur, in lesser degree, until the "representation" fades into "scene," and Mamie and Strether's dialogue begins.

Lapses and shifts of this nature may be thought relatively minor; and it might have been difficult for James or anyone else at this time completely to avoid them. But the point is that they are present, and pervasively so, and that they are inconsistencies in his method.

James's deviations from his ideal technique, furthermore, also involve shifts of point of view from Strether's to other characters'. These are the most difficult of all to perceive, for it is here that the Master's art of concealment is most splendidly subtle. These shifts are not abundant, and they do not last long; but they too are nonetheless present.

Even Lubbock, for all his enthusiastic claims, made one concession of "an insidious shifting . . . artfully contrived," whereby we get a little more than "Strether's vision and the play of his mind." These shifts occasionally occur in "the *scenic* episodes," such as the colloquies with Miss Gostrey, wherein "Strether's point of view still reigns; the only eyes in the matter are still his, there is no sight of the man himself as his companion sees him." Still, "we seem to have edged away from Strether's consciousness. He sees, and we with him; but when he *talks* it is almost as though we were outside him and away from him altogether." Thus it is "as though he had almost become what he cannot be, an objective figure for the reader (161, 165–67).

Often, however, though the point of view is *apparently* Strether's, there occur cunning hints of a momentary shift. Most frequently it is by indirection, with the help of an "as if" or an "appeared": "There could be no better example—and [Miss Gostrey] appeared to note it with high amusement . . ." (155), and "She spoke ever so gently and as if with all fear of wounding him . . ." (211). The most striking example of this indirection is the entire Chapter XXXI, describing Strether's meeting with Chad and Mme. de Vionnet in the country. Except for some highly intrusive editorial chit-chat (384–86, already noted above), the point of view seems to be Strether's; yet to achieve the full ironical drama of the episode James must have thought that he should inform the reader how Chad and his lady feel. A few excerpts will suggest how James lets the point of view swim for a moment toward the lovers without ever quite seeming to relinquish its tie to Strether, except in the last quotation:

> [The boat] had . . . come . . . near enough for Strether to fancy the lady in the stern had, for some reason, taken account of his being there to watch them. She had remarked on it sharply, yet her companion had not turned round; it was in fact as if our friend had felt her bid him keep still. . . . (382)

> Strether became aware . . . that her recognition had been even stranger for the pair in the boat, that her immediate impulse had been to control it, and that she was quickly and intensely debating with Chad the risk of betrayal. (383) Strether saw how she had perceived in a flash that they couldn't quite look to going back there under his nose [i.e., to their "quiet retreat"]; though, as he gouged deeper into the matter, he was somewhat surprised, as Chad likewise had been, at the uprising of this scruple. He seemed even to divine that she had entertained it rather for Chad than for herself, and that, as the young man had lacked the chance to enlighten her, she had had to go on with it, he meanwhile mistaking her motive. (388)

Now and then, as in the next chapter, the focus is so hazy that the reader cannot be quite sure that, for a few lines, the point of view has not in fact become that of the other character:

> She [Mme. de Vionnet] knew she hadn't really thrown dust in his eyes; this, the previous night, before they separated, had practically passed between them; and, as she had sent for him to see what the difference thus made for him might amount to, so he was conscious at the end of five minutes that he had been tried and tested. She had settled with Chad after he left them that she would, for her satisfaction, assure herself of this quantity, and Chad had, as usual, let her have her way. (399)

Surely in cases like these James has impregnated our friend with a scarcely cogent clairvoyance, a rarefied ability to sense matters, that seems hardly credible, especially in one who took so long to become aware of how things really stood between Chad and his charmer.

Sometimes, however, there is no possible ambiguity: the point of view unmistakably slips from Strether. Often it is momentary, as when Mrs. Pocock "had already said more than she had quite expected" (342). But often, too, the shift is more consequential. Of Miss Gostrey James writes: "She had time to take in her companion's face; and with it, as such things were easy for her, she took all in"; and, a little later, "But by that time Miss Gostrey was convinced that she didn't want to be better than Strether" (32). Speaking of the Newsomes' indefinite article, James remarks that Strether's "postponements" of naming it "made her wonder—wonder if the article referred to anything bad." Then, after noting that Strether "never *was* to tell her," James continues: "He actually never did so, . . . her desire for the information dropped, and her attitude to the question converted itself into a positive calculation of ignorance. In ignorance she could humor her fancy, and that proved a useful freedom . . ." (42–43; see also 46–47, 51, 98, 411).

On several occasions the point of view is Chad's—for example: "Chad Newsome was doubtless to be struck . . . with the sharpness of their opposition . . . ; he was to remember . . . how Waymarsh came with him and with Strether . . ." (245). Or, perhaps feeling the need for a shift, James maintains apparent consistency by the use of speculative phraseology: "there was . . . a pause in which the younger companion [Chad] might have been taken as weighing again the delicacy of his . . . promising the elder some provision. . . . This, however, he presumably thought best not to do . . ." (370). And once James's implication of point of view is so ambiguous that most readers would assume that he has indeed boldly switched to Chad's.

Strether has just told Chad he would be a brute if he forsook his mistress:

> When once he had heard himself say it he felt that his message had never before been spoken. . . . Chad showed no shade of embarrassment, but had . . . been troubled for him after their meeting in the country; had had fears and doubts on the subject of his comfort. He was disturbed . . . only for him, and had positively gone away to ease him off, to let him down . . . the more gently. Seeing him now fairly jaded, he had come, with characteristic good-humor, all the way to meet him, and what Strether thereupon . . . made out was that he would abound for him . . . in conscientious assurances." (420)

The art in such instances is often remarkably subtle, but occasionally it comes close to being essentially a dazzling technical trick that does not quite come off.

Henry James, it is hence fair to state, fulfilled rather less consistently than he thought his intention "of employing but one centre and keeping it all within [his] hero's compass," of projecting Strether's consciousness upon his experiences "from beginning to end without intermission or deviation," and of availing himself of "Strether's sense of these things, and Strether's only . . . for showing them." [3] The authorial intrusion and the shifts of point of view are sufficiently abundant to modify his claim. Moreover, unqualified critical claims like those quoted earlier clearly need toning down. The author has not completely withdrawn; Strether's thought does not tell *all* "its own story"; the subject does not consist "entirely" of his impressions; we do see many interpositions of authorial visions; James does not "most carefully [refrain] from using his knowledge"; and, far from having vanished, the author is very much present, frequently "addressing us" and "reporting his impression to the reader."

James, in all likelihood, was still so close to the conventions of nineteenth-century fiction that he could never quite eschew their besetting manners and methods; and so in *The Ambassadors* he continued to assume to a considerable degree the prerogatives of intrusive authorship he had enjoyed in his earlier works, with at least most of the editorial rights and privileges thereunto appertaining. Such variations from his ideal, however, are not merely noteworthy in themselves, for they offer hitherto neglected evidence of his struggle,

---

[3] In 1912, writing to Hugh Walpole of "poor dear Strether's discipline, development, and general history," James said: "All of it that is of my subject seems to me given—given by dramatic projection, as all the rest is given: how can you say I do anything so foul and abject as to 'state'? You deserve that I should condemn you to read the book over once again!" (*The Letters of Henry James,* ed. Percy Lubbock, New York, 1920, II, 245).

in what he believed to be his finest work, to master the art of his craft. At the end of his Preface to *The Ambassadors,* he observes that "the Novel remains still . . . the most independent, most elastic, and most prodigious of literary forms." And with James, as we have seen, it retained, for all his mastery, much of its independence.

The First Paragraph of *The Ambassadors:*
An Explication

by Ian Watt

I

Strether's first question, when he reached the hotel, was
about his friend; yet on his learning that Waymarsh was
apparently not to arrive till evening he was not wholly disconcerted. A telegram from him bespeaking a room 'only
5   if not noisy,' reply paid, was produced for the inquirer at
the office, so that the understanding they should meet at
Chester rather than at Liverpool remained to that extent
sound. The same secret principle, however, that had
prompted Strether not absolutely to desire Waymarsh's
10   presence at the dock, that had led him thus to postpone
for a few hours his enjoyment of it, now operated to make
him feel he could still wait without disappointment. They
would dine together at the worst, and, with all respect to
dear old Waymarsh—if not even, for that matter, to him-
15   self—there was little fear that in the sequel they shouldn't
see enough of each other. The principle I have just mentioned as operating had been, with the most newly disembarked of the two men, wholly instinctive—the fruit
of a sharp sense that, delightful as it would be to find him-
20   self looking, after so much separation, into his comrade's
face, his business would be a trifle bungled should he
simply arrange for this countenance to present itself to the
nearing steamer as the first 'note' of Europe. Mixed with
everything was the apprehension, already, on Strether's
25   part, that it would, at best, throughout, prove the note of
Europe in quite a sufficient degree.[1]

"The First Paragraph of The Ambassadors: *An Explication" by Ian Watt. From*
Essays in Criticism, X *(July, 1960), pp. 254–68; revised version appears in* The Ambassadors, *Norton Critical Edition, ed. S. P. Rosenbaum, pp. 468–81. Reprinted by
permission of the author and* Essays in Criticism.

[1] Henry James, *The Ambassadors* (Revised Collected Edition, Macmillan: Lon-

It seems a fairly ordinary sort of prose, but for its faint air of elaborate portent; and on second reading its general quality reminds one of what Strether is later to observe—approvingly—in Maria Gostrey: an effect of "expensive, subdued suitability." There's certainly nothing particularly striking in the diction or syntax; none of the immediate drama or rich description that we often get at the beginning of novels; and certainly none of the sensuous concreteness that, until recently, was regarded as a chief criterion of good prose in our long post-imagistic phase: if anything, the passage is conspicuously un-sensuous and un-concrete, a little dull perhaps, and certainly not easy reading.

The difficulty isn't one of particularly long or complicated sentences: actually they're of fairly usual length: I make it an average of 41 words; a little, but not very much, longer than James' average of 35 (in Book 2, ch. 2. of *The Ambassadors*, according to R. W. Short's count, in his very useful article "The Sentence Structure of Henry James" (*American Literature*, XVIII [March 1946], 71–88.[2] The main cause of difficulty seems rather to come from what may be called the delayed specification of referents: "Strether" and "the hotel" and "his friend" are mentioned before we are told who or

---

don, 1923). Since there are a few variants that have a bearing on the argument, it seems desirable to give a collation of the main editions; P is the periodical publication (*The North American Review*, clxxvi, 1903); 1A the first American edition (Harper and Brothers, New York, 1903); 1E the first English edition (Methuen and Co., London, 1903); N.Y., the "New York Edition," New York and London, 1907–9 (the London Macmillan edition used the sheets of the American edition); CR the "Collected Revised Edition," London and New York, 1921–31 (which uses the text of the New York Edition). It should perhaps be explained that the most widely used editions in England and America make misleading claims about their text: the "Everyman" edition claims to use the text "of the revised Collected Edition," but actually follows the first English edition in the last variant; while the "Anchor" edition, claiming to be "a faithful copy of the text of the Methuen first edition," actually follows the first American edition, including the famous misplaced chapters.

1.5.   *reply paid* NY, CR; *with the answer paid* P, 1A, 1E.

1.5.   *inquirer* P, 1A, 1E, CR; *enquirer* NY.

1.6.   *understanding they* NY, CR; *understanding that they* P, 1A, 1E.

1.12.   *feel he* NY, CR; *feel that he* P, 1A, 1E.

1.15.   *shouldn't* CR; *shouldn't* NY; *should not* P, 1A, 1E.

1.17–8. *newly disembarked,* all eds. except P: *newly-disembarked.*

1.22.   *arrange for this countenance to present* NY, CR; *arrange that this countenance should present* P, 1A, 1E.

1.23.   *"note" of Europe* CR; *"note," for him, of Europe,* P, 1A, 1E; *"note," of Europe,* NY.

1.25.   *that it would* P, 1A, NY, CR; *that he would,* 1E.

[2] I am also indebted to the same author's "Henry James's World of Images," *PMLA*, LXVIII (December, 1953), 943–60.

where they are. But this difficulty is so intimately connected with James's general narrative technique that it may be better to begin with purely verbal idiosyncrasies, which are more easily isolated. The most distinctive ones in the passage seem to be these: a preference for non-transitive verbs; many abstract nouns; much use of "that"; a certain amount of elegant variation to avoid piling up personal pronouns and adjectives such as "he," "his" and "him"; and the presence of a great many negatives and near-negatives.

By the preference for non-transitive verbs I mean three related habits: a great reliance on copulatives—"Strether's first question *was* about his friend"; "*was* apparently not to arrive": a frequent use of the passive voice—"*was* not wholly *disconcerted*"; "a telegram . . . *was produced*"; "his business *would be* a trifle *bungled*": and the employment of many intransitive verbs—"the understanding . . . remained . . . sound"; "the . . . principle . . . operated to." My count of all the verbs in the indicative would give a total of 14 passive, copulative or intransitive uses as opposed to only 6 transitive ones: and there are in addition frequent infinitive, participial, or gerundial uses of transitive verbs, in all of which the active nature of the subject-verb-and-object sequence is considerably abated—"on his learning"; "bespeaking a room"; "not absolutely to desire"; "led him thus to postpone."

This relative infrequency of transitive verbal usages in the passage is associated with the even more pronounced tendency towards using abstract nouns as subjects of main or subordinate clauses: "question"; "understanding"; "the same secret principle"; "the principle"; "his business." If one takes only the main clauses, there are four such abstract nouns as subjects, while only three main clauses have concrete and particular subjects ("he," or "they").[3]

I detail these features only to establish that in this passage, at least, there is a clear quantitative basis for the common enough view that James's late prose style is characteristically abstract; more explicitly, that the main grammatical subjects are very often nouns for mental ideas, "question," "principle," etc.; and that the verbs—because they are mainly used either non-transitively, or in infinitive, participial and gerundial forms,—tend to express states of being rather than particular finite actions affecting objects.

The main use of abstractions is to deal at the same time with many objects or events rather than single and particular ones: and we use verbs that denote states of being rather than actions for exactly the

---

[3] Sentences one and four are compound or multiple, but in my count I haven't included the second clause in the latter—"there was little fear": though if we can talk of the clause having a subject it's an abstract one—"fear."

same reason—their much more general applicability. But in this passage, of course, James isn't in the ordinary sense making abstract or general statements; it's narrative, not expository prose; what need exploring, therefore, are the particular literary imperatives which impose on his style so many of the verbal and syntactical qualities of abstract and general discourse; of expository rather than narrative prose.

Consider the first sentence. The obvious narrative way of making things particular and concrete would presumably be "When Strether reached the hotel, he first asked 'Has Mr. Waymarsh arrived yet?'" Why does James say it the way he does? One effect is surely that, instead of a sheer stated event, we get a very special view of it; the mere fact that actuality has been digested into reported speech—the question "was about his friend"—involves a narrator to do the job, to interpret the action, and also a presumed audience that he does it for: and by implication, the heat of the action itself must have cooled off somewhat for the translation and analysis of the events into this form of statement to have had time to occur. Lastly, making the subject of the sentence "question" rather than "he," has the effect of subordinating the particular actor, and therefore the particular act, to a much more general perspective: mental rather than physical, and subjective rather than objective; "question" is a word which involves analysis of a physical event into terms of meaning and intention: it involves, in fact, both Strether's mind and the narrator's. The narrator's, because he interprets Strether's act: if James had sought the most concrete method of taking us into Strether's mind—"'Has Mr. Waymarsh come yet?' I at once asked"—he would have obviated the need for the implied external categoriser of Strether's action. But James disliked the "mere platitude of statement" involved in first-person narrative; partly, presumably, because it would merge Strether's consciousness into the narrative, and not isolate it for the reader's inspection. For such isolation, a more expository method is needed: no confusion of subject and object, as in first-person narration, but a narrator forcing the reader to pay attention to James's primary objective—Strether's mental and subjective state.

The "multidimensional" quality of the narrative, with its continual implication of a community of three minds—Strether's, James's, and the reader's—isn't signalled very obviously until the fourth sentence—"The principle I have just mentioned as operating . . ."; but it's already been established tacitly in every detail of diction and structure, and it remains pervasive. One reason for the special demand James's fictional prose makes on our attention is surely that there are always at least three levels of development—all of them subjective: the characters' awareness of events: the narrator's seeing of them; and our own trailing perception of the relation between these two.

The primary location of the narrative in a mental rather than a physical continuum gives the narrative a great freedom from the restrictions of particular time and place. Materially, we are, of course, in Chester, at the hotel—characteristically "the hotel" because a fully particularised specification—"The Pied Bull Inn" say—would be an irrelevant brute fact which would distract attention from the mental train of thought we are invited to partake in. But actually we don't have any pressing sense of time and place: we feel ourselves to be spectators, rather specifically, of Strether's thought processes, which easily and imperceptibly range forwards and backwards both in time and space. Sentence three, for example, begins in the past, at the Liverpool dock; sentence four looks forward to the reunion later that day, and to its many sequels: such transitions of time and place are much easier to effect when the main subjects of the sentences are abstract: a "principle" exists independently of its context.

The multiplicity of relations—between narrator and object, and between the ideas in Strether's mind—held in even suspension throughout the narrative, is presumably the main explanation for the number of "thats" in the passage, as well as of the several examples of elegant variation. There are 9 "thats"—only two of them demonstrative and the rest relative pronouns (or conjunctions or particles if you prefer those terms); actually there were no less than three more of them in the first edition, which James removed from the somewhat more colloquial and informal New York edition; while there are several other "thats" implied—in "the principle [that] I have just mentioned," for instance.

The number of "thats" follows from two habits already noted in the passage. "That" characteristically introduces relative clauses dealing not with persons but with objects, including abstractions; and it is also used to introduce reported speech—"on his learning that Waymarsh"—not "Mr. Waymarsh isn't here." Both functions are combined in the third sentence where we get a triple definition of a timeless idea based on the report of three chronologically separate events "the same secret principle, however, that had prompted Strether not absolutely to desire Waymarsh's presence at the dock, that had led him thus to postpone for a few hours his enjoyment of it, now operated to make him feel that he could still wait without disappointment."

Reported rather than direct speech also increases the pressure towards elegant variation: the use, for example, in sentence 1 of "his friend," where in direct speech it would be "Mr. Waymarsh" (and the reply—"*He* hasn't come yet"). In the second sentence—"a telegram

. . . was produced for the inquirer"—"inquirer" is needed because "him" has already been used for Waymarsh just above; of course, "the inquirer" is logical enough after the subject of the first sentence has been an abstract noun—"question"; and the epithet also gives James an opportunity for underlining the ironic distance and detachment with which we are invited to view his dedicated "inquirer," Strether. Later, when Strether is "the most newly disembarked of the two men," we see how both elegant variation and the grammatical subordination of physical events are related to the general Jamesian tendency to present characters and actions on a plane of abstract categorisation; the mere statement, "Mr. Waymarsh had already been in England for [so many] months," would itself go far to destroy the primarily mental continuum in which the paragraph as a whole exists.

The last general stylistic feature of the passage to be listed above was the use of negative forms. There are 6 "noes" or "nots" in the first 4 sentences; four implied negatives—"postpone"; "without disappointment"; "at the worst"; "there was little fear": and two qualifications that modify positiveness of affirmation—"not wholly," and "to that extent." This abundance of negatives has no doubt several functions: it enacts Strether's tendency to hesitation and qualification; it puts the reader into the right judicial frame of mind; and it has the further effect of subordinating concrete events to their mental reflection; "Waymarsh was not to arrive," for example, is not a concrete statement of a physical event: it is subjective—because it implies an expectation in Strether's mind (which was not fulfilled); and it has an abstract quality—because while Waymarsh's arriving would be particular and physical, his *not* arriving is an idea, a non-action. More generally, James's great use of negatives or near-negatives may also, perhaps, be regarded as part of his subjective and abstractive tendency: there are no negatives in nature but only in the human consciousness.

II

The most obvious grammatical features of what Richard Chase has called Henry James's "infinitely syntactical language" (*The American Novel and its Tradition*, New York, 1957), can, then, be shown to reflect the essential imperatives of his narrative point of view; and they could therefore lead into a discussion of the philosophical qualities of his mind, as they are discussed, for example, by Dorothea Krook in her notable article "The Method of the Later Works of Henry James" (*London Magazine*, I [1954], 55–70); our passage surely exemplifies James's power "to generalise to the furthest limit the particulars of experience," and with it the characteristic way in which both his "perceptions of the world itself and his perceptions of the logic of his perceptions of the world . . . happen simultaneously, are the parts of a single comprehensive experience." Another aspect of the connection between James's metaphysic and his method as a novelist has inspired a stimulating stylistic study—Carlo Izzo's "Henry James, Scrittore Sintattico" (*Studi Americani,* II [1956], 127–42). The connection between thought and style finds its historical perspective in John Henry Raleigh's illuminating study "Henry James: The Poetics of Empiricism" (*PMLA,* LXVI [1951], 107–23), which establishes connections between Lockean epistemology and James's extreme, almost anarchic, individualism; while this epistemological preoccupation, which is central to Quentin Anderson's view of how James worked out his father's cosmology in fictional terms (*The American Henry James,* New Brunswick, 1957), also leads towards another large general question, the concern with "point of view," which became a crucial problem in the history and criticism of fiction under the influence of the sceptical relativism of the late nineteenth-century.

In James's case, the problem is fairly complicated. He may be classed as an "Impressionist," concerned, that is, to show not so much the events themselves, but the impressions which they make on the characters. But James's continual need to generalise and place and order, combined with his absolute demand for a point of view that would be plastic enough to allow him freedom for the formal "architectonics" of the novelist's craft, eventually involved him in a very idiosyncratic kind of multiple Impressionism: idiosyncratic because the dual presence of Strether's consciousness and that of the narrator, who translates what he sees there into more general terms, makes the narrative point of view both intensely individual and yet ultimately social.

Another possible direction of investigation would be to show that the abstractness and indirection of James's style are essentially the result of this characteristic multiplicity of his vision. There is, for example, the story reported by Edith Wharton that after his first stroke James told Lady Prothero that "in the very act of falling . . . he heard in the room a voice which was distinctly, it seemed, not his own, saying: 'So here it is at last, the distinguished thing.' " James, apparently, could not but see even his own most fateful personal experience, except as evoked by some other observer's voice in terms of the long historical and literary tradition of death. Carlo Izzo regards this tendency as typical of the Alexandrian style, where there is a marked disparity between the rich inheritance of the means of literary expression, and the meaner creative world which it is used to express; but the defence of the Jamesian habit of mind must surely be that what the human vision shares with that of animals is presumably the perception of concrete images, not the power to conceive universals: such was Aristotle's notion of man's distinguishing capacity. The universals in the present context are presumably the awareness that behind every petty individual circumstance there ramifies an endless network of general moral, social and historical relations. Henry James's style can therefore be seen as a supremely civilised effort to relate every event and every moment of life to the full complexity of its circumambient conditions.

Obviously James's multiple awareness can go too far; and in the later novels it often poses the special problem that we do not quite know whether the awareness implied in a given passage is the narrator's or that of his character. Most simply, a pronoun referring to the subject of a preceding clause is always liable to give trouble if one hasn't been very much aware of what the grammatical subject of that preceding clause was; in the last sentence of the paragraph, for example, "the apprehension, already, on Strether's part, that . . . it would, at best, . . . prove the 'note' of Europe," "it" refers to Waymarsh's countenance: but this isn't at first obvious; which is no doubt why, in his revision of the periodical version for the English edition James replaced "it" by "he"—simpler, grammatically, but losing some of the ironic visual precision of the original. More seriously, because the narrator's consciousness and Strether's are both present, we often don't know whose mental operations and evaluative judgments are involved in particular cases. We pass, for instance, from the objective analysis of sentence 3 where the analytic terminology of "the same secret principle" must be the responsibility of the narrator, to what must be a verbatim quotation of Strether's mind in sentence 4: "with all respect to dear old Waymarsh" is obviously Strether's licensed familiarity.

But although the various difficulties of tense, voice, and reference require a vigilance of attention in the reader which some have found too much to give, they are not in themselves very considerable: and what perhaps is much more in need of attention is how the difficulties arising from the multiplicity of points of view don't by any means prevent James from ordering all the elements of his narrative style into an amazingly precise means of expression: and it is this positive, and in the present case, as it seems to me, triumphant, mastery of the difficulties which I want next to consider.

Our passage is not, I think, James either at his most memorable or at his most idiosyncratic: *The Ambassadors* is written with considerable sobriety and has, for example, little of the vivid and direct style of the early part of *The Wings of the Dove,* or of the happy symbolic complexities of *The Golden Bowl*. Still, the passage is fairly typical of the later James; and I think it can be proved that all or at least nearly all the idiosyncrasies of diction or syntax in the present passage are fully justified by the particular emphases they create.

The most flagrant eccentricity of diction is presumably that where James writes "the most newly disembarked of the two men" (lines 16–17). "Most" may very well be a mere slip; and it must certainly seem indefensible to any one who takes it as an absolute rule that the comparative must always be used when only two items are involved.[4] But a defence is at least possible. "Most newly disembarked" means something rather different from "more newly disembarked." James, it may be surmised, did not want to compare the recency of the two men's arrival, but to inform us that Strether's arrival was "very" or as we might say, "most" recent; the use of the superlative also had the advantage of suggesting the long and fateful tradition of transatlantic disembarcations in general.

The reasons for the other main syntactical idiosyncrasies in the passage are much clearer. In the first part of the opening sentence, for example, the separation of subject—"question"—from the verb—"was"—by the longish temporal clause "when he reached the hotel," is no doubt a dislocation of normal sentence structure; but, of course, "Strether" must be the first word of the novel: while, even more important, the delayed placing of the temporal clause, forces a pause after "question" and thus gives it a very significant resonance. Similarly with the last sentence; it has several peculiarities, of which the placing of "throughout" seems the most obvious. The sentence has three parts: the first and last are comparatively straightforward, but the middle is a massed block of portentous qualifications: "Mixed with everything was the apprehension—already, on Strether's part, that he would, at best, throughout,—prove the note of Europe in quite a sufficient degree." The echoing doom started by the connotation of "apprehension"—reverberates through "already," ("much more to come later") "on Strether's part" ("even he knows") and "at best" ("the worst has been envisaged, too"); but it is the final collapse of the terse rhythm of the parenthesis that isolates the rather awkwardly placed "throughout," and thus enables James to sound the fine full fatal note; there is no limit to the poignant eloquence of "throughout." It was this effect, of course, which dictated the preceding inversion which places "apprehension" not at the start of the sentence, but in the middle where, largely freed from its syntactical nexus, it may be directly exposed to its salvos of qualification.

---

[4] Though consider *Rasselas*, ch. xxviii: "Both conditions may be bad, but they cannot both be worst."

The mockingly fateful emphasis on "throughout" tells us, if nothing had before, that James's tone is in the last analysis ironic, comic, or better, as I shall try to suggest, humorous. The general reasons for this have already been suggested. To use Maynard Mack's distinction (in his Preface to *Joseph Andrews,* Rinehart Editions, New York, 1948), "the comic artist subordinates the presentation of life as experience, where the relationship between ourselves and the characters experiencing it is a primary one, to the presentation of life as a spectacle, where the primary relation is between himself and us as onlookers." In the James passage, the primacy of the relation between the narrator and the reader has already been noted, as has its connection with the abstraction of the diction, which brings home the distance between the narrator and Strether. Of course, the application of abstract diction to particular persons always tends towards irony,[5] because it imposes a dual way of looking at them: few of us can survive being presented as general representatives of humanity.

The paragraph, of course, is based on one of the classic contradictions in psychological comedy—Strether's reluctance to admit to himself that he has very mixed feelings about his friend: and James develops this with the narrative equivalent of *commedia dell'arte* technique: virtuoso feats of ironic balance, comic exaggeration, and deceptive hesitation conduct us on a complicated progress towards the foreordained illumination.

In structure, to begin with, the six sentences form three groups of two: each pair of them gives one aspect of Strether's delay; and they are arranged in an ascending order of complication so that the fifth sentence—72 words—is almost twice as long as any other, and is succeeded by the final sentence, the punch line, which is noticeably the shortest—26 words. The development of the ideas is as controlled as the sentence structure. Strether is obviously a man with an enormous sense of responsibility about personal relationships; so his first question is about his friend. That loyal *empressement,* however, is immediately checked by the balanced twin negatives that follow: "on his learning that Waymarsh *was not* to arrive till evening, he *was not* wholly disconcerted": one of the diagnostic elements of irony, surely, is hyperbole qualified with mock-scrupulousness, such as we get in "not wholly disconcerted." Why there are limits to Lambert Strether's consternation is to transpire in the next sentence; Waymarsh's telegram bespeaking a room "only if not noisy" is a laconic suggestion of that inarticulate worthy's habitually gloomy expectations—from his past experiences of the indignities of European hotel noise we adum-

---

[5] As I have argued in "The Ironic Tradition in Augustan Prose from Swift to Johnson," *Restoration and Augustan Prose* (Los Angeles, 1957).

brate the notion that the cost of their friendly *rencontre* may be his sleeping in the street. In the second part of the sentence we have another similar, though more muted, hint: "the understanding that they should meet in Chester rather than at Liverpool remained to that extent sound"; "to that extent," no doubt, but to *any other?*—echo seems to answer "No."

In the second group of sentences we are getting into Strether's mind, and we have been prepared to relish the irony of its ambivalences. The negatived hyperbole of "not absolutely to desire," turns out to mean "postpone"; and, of course, a voluntarily postponed "enjoyment" itself denotes a very modified rapture, although Strether's own consciousness of the problem is apparently no further advanced than that "he could still wait without disappointment." Comically loyal to what he would like to feel, therefore, we have him putting in the consoling reflection that "they would dine together at the worst"; and the ambiguity of "at the worst" is followed by the equally dubious thought: "there was little fear that in the sequel they shouldn't see enough of each other." That they should, in fact, see too much of each other; but social decorum and Strether's own loyalties demand that the outrage of the open statement be veiled in the obscurity of formal negation.

By the time we arrive at the climactic pair of sentences, we have been told enough for more ambitious effects to be possible. The twice-mentioned "secret principle," it appears, is actually wholly "instinctive" (line 17); but in other ways Strether is almost ludicrously self-conscious. The qualified hyperbole of "his business would be a trifle bungled," underlined as it is by the alliteration, prepares us for a half-realised image which amusingly defines Strether's sense of his role: he sees himself, it appears, as the stage-manager of an enterprise in which his solemn obligations as an implicated friend are counterbalanced by his equally ceremonious sense that due decorums must also be attended to when he comes face to face with another friend of long ago—no less a person than Europe. It is, of course, silly of him, as James makes him acknowledge in the characteristic italicising of "the 'note' of Europe";[6] but still, he does have a comically ponderous sense of protocol which leads him to feel that "his business would be a trifle bungled" should he simply arrange for this countenance to present itself to the nearing steamer as the first "note" of Europe. The steamer, one imagines, would not have turned hard astern at the proximity of Waymarsh's sacred rage; but Strether's fitness for ambassadorial functions is defined by his thinking in terms of "arranging"

[6] See George Knox, "James's Rhetoric of Quotes," *College English*, XVII (1956), 293-97.

for a certain countenance at the docks to give just the right symbolic greeting.

Strether's notion of what Europe demands also shows us the force of his aesthetic sense. But in the last sentence the metaphor, though it remains equally self-conscious, changes its mode of operation from the dramatic, aesthetic, and diplomatic, to something more scientific: for, although ten years ago I should not have failed to point out, and my readers would not, I suppose, have failed to applaud, the ambiguity of "prove," it now seems to me that we must choose between its two possible meanings. James may be using "prove" to mean that Waymarsh's face will "turn out to be" the "note of Europe"—for Strether. But "prove" in this sense is intransitive, and "to be" would have to be supplied; it therefore seems more likely that James is using "prove" in the older sense of "to test": Waymarsh is indeed suited to the role of being the sourly acid test of the siren songs of Europe "in quite a sufficient degree," as Strether puts it with solemn but arch understanding.

The basic development structure of the passage, then, is one of progressive and yet artfully delayed clarification; and this pattern is also typical of James's general novelistic method. The reasons for this are suggested in the Preface to *The Princess Casamassima,* where James deals with the problem of maintaining a balance between the intelligence a character must have to be interesting, and the bewilderment which is nevertheless an essential condition of the novel's having surprise, development, and tension: "It seems probable that if we were never bewildered there would never be a story to tell about us."

In the first paragraph of *The Ambassadors* James apprises us both of his hero's supreme qualities and of his associated limitations. Strether's delicate critical intelligence is often blinkered by a highly vulnerable mixture of moral generosity towards others combined with an obsessive sense of personal inadequacy; we see the tension in relation to Waymarsh, as later we are to see it in relation to all his other friends; and we understand, long before Strether, how deeply it bewilders him; most poignantly about the true nature of Chad, Madame de Vionnet—and himself.

This counterpoint of intelligence and bewilderment is, of course, another reason for the split narrative point of view we've already noted: we and the narrator are inside Strether's mind, and yet we are also outside it, knowing more about Strether than he knows about himself. This is the classic posture of irony. Yet I think that to insist too exclusively on the ironic function of James's narrative point of view would be mistaken.

Irony has lately been enshrined as the supreme deity in the critical pantheon: but, I wonder, is there really anything so wonderful about being distant and objective? Who wants to see life only or mainly in intellectual terms? In art as in life we no doubt can have need of intellectual distance as well as of emotional commitment; but the uninvolvement of the artist surely doesn't go very far without the total involvement of the person; or, at least, without a deeper human involvement than irony customarily establishes. One could, I suppose, call the aesthetically perfect balance between distance and involvement, open or positive irony: but I'm not sure that humour isn't a better word, especially when the final balance is tipped in favour of involvement, of ultimate commitment to the characters; and I hope that our next critical movement will be the New Gelastics.

At all events, although the first paragraph alone doesn't allow the point to be established fully here, it seems to me that James's attitude to Strether is better described as humorous than ironical; we must learn like Maria Gostrey, to see him "at last all comically, all tragically." James's later novels in general are most intellectual; but they are also, surely, his most compassionate: and in this particular paragraph Strether's dilemma is developed in such a way that we feel for him even more than we smile at him. This balance of intention, I think, probably explains why James keeps his irony so quiet in tone: we must be aware of Strether's "secret" ambivalence towards Waymarsh, but not to the point that his unawareness of it would verge on fatuity; and our controlling sympathy for the causes of Strether's ambivalence turns what might have been irony into something closer to what Constance Rourke characterises as James's typical "low-keyed humor of defeat" (*American Humor,* 1931).

That James's final attitude is humorous rather than ironic is further suggested by the likeness of the basic structural technique of the paragraph to that of the funny story—the incremental involvement in an endemic human perplexity which can only be resolved by laughter's final acceptance of contradiction and absurdity. We don't, in the end, see Strether's probing hesitations mainly as an ironic indication by James of mankind's general muddlement; we find it, increasingly, a touching example of how, despite all their inevitable incongruities and shortcomings, human ties remain only, but still, human.

Here it is perhaps James's very slowness and deliberation throughout the narrative which gives us our best supporting evidence: greater love hath no man than hearing his friend out patiently.

The Text of *The Ambassadors*

by Leon Edel

Six editions of Henry James's *The Ambassadors,* five paperback and one hardcover, are now in print.[1] Of these, four paperback editions have been published during the present year. Thus the novel that James judged to be "quite the best, 'all round,' of all my productions," [2] is now also the one most generally available. This may be held to be a symptom either of public interest or of publishing taste—or of both. For *The Ambassadors* has always been considered a "difficult" novel, and even its author conceded that a reader had to take the book "very easily and gently: read five pages a day—be even as deliberate as that —but *don't break the thread.*" [3] Certainly it can be said of it that, during its first half century, it has had a limited public save in the universities. Its rise to the eminence of a classic has hardly been as sensational as that of *Moby Dick.* The book has, indeed, imposed itself upon the literary conscience of America and England only by degrees. Yet it has emerged from its comparative obscurity—and often obloquy—and its arrival in the great paperback democracy may provide a study of changing literary taste and of the whole question of "modernity" in fiction.

A great anomaly, however, is to be found in certain textual problems in this novel. These were raised as far back as 1950, when a student discovered that two chapters in the book had been published in reverse order, in "all available editions." [4] Scholarship did not then

---

"The Text of The Ambassadors*" by Leon Edel. From the* Harvard Library Bulletin, *XIV (Autumn, 1960), 453–60. Reprinted by permission of the author and the* Harvard Library Bulletin.

[1] The paperbacks are: Anchor, ed. Robert W. Stallman, 1958; Signet, ed. Stallman, 1960; Fawcett, ed. Bergen Evans, 1960; Rinehart, ed. Frederick W. Dupee, 1960; Riverside, ed. Leon Edel, 1960. The hardcover is in the Harper *Modern Classics* series, where it has been in print for many years.

[2] Preface to *The Ambassadors,* New York Edition, 1909, p. vii.

[3] *The Selected Letters of Henry James,* ed. Leon Edel, 2nd ed. (New York, 1960), pp. 189–90.

[4] See below, p. [94].

adequately clear up the textual question and identify the different texts for us. Two texts of *The Ambassadors* have appeared since then, duplicating the original error. And the present proliferation of editions offers three different textual versions. One would think a little more highly of our surfeited American studies in the colleges if we had been given a reasonably prompt comparison of all the texts to determine which was the definitive, as well as a study of the various revisions made by James in the progress of the work from serial to volume.[5] I have used the word "anomaly" because we live in an era of "explication" of text, and one would think that our scholars and critics would determine first what their text is, before they start their explications. Such scholarship, it seems to me, would be more valuable than a good deal of the chronic search for hidden "levels" of meaning, and the constant avoidance by certain schools of criticism of the apparent, the real, the concrete, for the hypothetical, the "probable," and the mythical.[6]

It is not my intention in this article to examine the texts of *The Ambassadors*. The general textual problem was outlined by myself and my collaborator Dan H. Laurence in *A Bibliography of Henry James*.[7] Nor do I wish to renew the ten-year-old controversy surrounding the question of the misplaced chapter. The purpose of this article is essentially to amplify a few points I have made earlier, particularly since variant texts of the novel are now generally available.

I

Let us rehearse briefly the history of the strange error that resulted in the misplacing of a chapter in *The Ambassadors*. (It is more accurate to speak of what happened as a "misplacing" of a single chapter than a "reversal" of chapters.) In 1901, when Henry James completed the book, he wrote to his agent, J. B. Pinker, announcing that he was withholding material from the serialization of the novel, which was to run through twelve monthly numbers of the *North American Review*.[8]

---

[5] I know of two graduate students who have at last undertaken this task.

[6] Such as the recent speculation by John A. Clair in "*The American*: A Reinterpretation," *PMLA*, LXXIV (1959), 613–18, as to whether Madame de Cintré is the illegitimate daughter of the housekeeper, as if the novelist would want to conceal relevant data from his reader.

[7] London, 1957, pp. 123–26.

[8] The James letters to Pinker are used by kind permission of the Yale University Library. The material here is drawn from letters of 9, 22 May, 6, 10 July, 13, 26 August, 4, 13 September, all of 1901.

This material, he said, would be reinserted in the book form. Being thoroughly familiar with the hazards of publication, James expressed this in words that left no room for doubt. He wanted, he said, to place it "on witnessed record that I formally ask for duplicate *Proofs* of the serial and that I as formally give warning that the volume is to contain a small quantity of additional material." How well founded this precaution was, may be judged by the fact that a few weeks before publication of the American edition James was still asking for the duplicate proof. "The Harpers," he wrote to his agent on 13 August 1903, "have been of a mortal slowness in sending me proof of the last third of the Book." [9] But, he added, he had finally received and read the page proofs. What we do not know is whether these pages contained the inserted and misplaced chapter. If they did, James could be held guilty of a grave oversight. However, we do know that he was an inveterate proof reader and a demanding one; he trusted neither publisher nor printer, as his precautions show. Had he found the error we know that Harper would have heard of it promptly, for James never hesitated to cable to his trans-Atlantic publishers in such matters. Obviously he did not see the mistake. And it is possible that the insertion had not yet been made.

We know also that at the time of the reading of the Harper proof James was still seeing the last galleys of the serial, and at the same time reading proof of the English edition. The reading and rereading of the same novel may have ended in a kind of visual inertia; but to this we can oppose the possibility that it may have also heightened the chances of discovering the error. In the absence of accurate data such speculation is, however, fruitless. The greatest weight must be assigned to the simple fact that the English edition, which James saw through the press, came out in September 1903 with all the chapters in their proper order, while the American edition, issued in November, had one chapter out of place. James apparently had not been informed that the American edition would appear so promptly, for he wrote to his brother William, on November 26th:

> I am afraid you will think me very stingy with my books when it comes over me that I have neglected till this hour to ask the Harpers to send you a copy of the *Ambassadors,* lately published (I believe,)—for I am much in the dark about it. It has been out *here* some weeks. I will have it done now if it be not too late (I hear of their sending *out* to me 6 copies; which—in the American edition—I don't want here.)

On December 2nd he announced to William: "Six copies of the American 'Ambassadors' have tumbled over upon me here, & I send one of

[9] *Selected Letters,* pp. 97–98.

them back to you by bookpost, in spite of what I fear are the jealous American P. O. (fiscal) botherations about the same." [10]

Shortly after the English edition appeared, James wrote to Mrs. Humphry Ward alluding to some "fearful, though much patched over fault or weakness" in the book, "which, however, I seem to see no one has noticed, and which nothing will induce me *now* ever to reveal—or at least till some one does spot it!" [11] This could, on the face of it, be an allusion to the misplaced chapter. It is doubtful, however, whether James would slough off so significant an error in this fashion. In James's own copy of the Methuen edition, preserved in the Harvard College Library (he does not seem to have kept a copy of the Harper edition), there are only two corrections in his hand, in ink. On page 132 (Chapter IX),[12] beginning five lines from the bottom, the printed version reads: "Little Bilham had got up as if the transaction with the waiter had been a signal . . ." Here James crossed out "had been" and substituted "were." This change was not incorporated by him in the New York Edition. On page 183 (Chapter XIII),[13] in the fifth paragraph, the printed text reads: " 'It isn't at all necessary you should understand it; it will do quite well enough if you simply remember him.' " The word "him" was altered by the novelist to "it." This change was incorporated in the New York Edition.

These corrections, however, do not suggest a "much patched over fault or weakness" in the book, and it is possible that James may be speaking of the discrepancy in the time scheme of the novel, resulting from the misplaced chapter, without having noticed that the chapter itself was in the wrong place. Yet this seems hardly likely, since Mrs. Ward would almost certainly have been reading the English edition, where the chapters are in proper sequence. James seemed indeed to consider the error of which he speaks as integral to the book, regardless of edition. Consequently we can only speculate about his statement: we have insufficient data to reach any conclusion.

II

It will be useful to list the different publications of *The Ambassadors* during James's life to indicate what occurred:

(1) The serial in the *North American Review,* January to Decem-

---

[10] Both quotations from unpublished letters in the Harvard College Library.

[11] Unpublished letter to Mrs Humphry Ward, 16 December 1903, courtesy of C. Waller Barrett.

[12] Book Fourth, Chapter II, of the New York Edition.

[13] Book Sixth, Chapter I, New York Edition.

ber 1903: this was published in 12 installments, each installment called
a "part," and consisting in all of 35 chapters.

(2) Methuen Edition: the first English edition, September 1903,
preceding by two months the American. James combined Chapters
XVIII and XIX of the serialization to form a new Chapter XVIII, and
inserted a new chapter XIX.[14] A further chapter, Chapter XXVIII,[15]
was inserted by James, as well as a long passage in Part Second (discussed below). Still another chapter was inserted in the final section
of the book. This is XXXV.[16] Thus three chapters in all were inserted, and almost half of another.[17]

(3) Harper Edition: New York, November 1903. The same chapters were inserted here as in the Methuen edition, but in Methuen
Chapters XVIII to XXI are placed in Part Eighth whereas in Harper
Chapter XVIII is in Part Seventh and Chapters XIX–XXI are in Part
Eighth. (XIX was the inserted chapter in this section.) In Harper
inserted Chapter XXVIII is numbered XXIX and made the second
chapter of Part Eleventh, whereas in Methuen it is the chapter that
concludes Part Tenth. It is here that the misplacing of the chapter
occurred. Chapter XXVIII in Harper is really XXIX; and XXIX is
really XXVIII. This is immediately apparent if the Methuen and
Harper editions are compared.

(4) New York Edition (Scribner): 1907–9. For this "definitive edition" James apparently used a paste-up of the Harper text. He altered
"Part" to "Book" throughout, and renumbered the chapters seriatim
in each section. This may explain why he overlooked the misplacing
of the chapter.

The obvious differences between the English and American editions
are thus a different division of chapters between certain of the parts,
and the misplacing of Chapter XXVIII, which was thereby assigned
a wrong number by Harper, resulting in the misplacing and misnum-
bering of Chapter XXIX.

III

Since James used carbon copies of the original typescript and made
corrections in these for part of his Methuen text certain differences
between it and the Harper text may be looked for. These are to be
found largely in the connective tissue by which James integrated his

[14] Book Eighth, Chapter I, New York Edition.
[15] Book Eleventh, Chapter II, New York Edition.
[16] Book Twelfth, Chapter IV, New York Edition.
[17] Not two chapters, as Dupee and Stallman say in their respective editions.

inserted portions with the rest of the book. An example of the differences between the two editions may be seen in the lengthy inserted passage in Part Second, the original Chapter V of the novel (and Chapter II, Book Second, in the New York Edition). This is the chapter in which Strether takes his stroll in the Luxembourg gardens and for the first time begins to experience the benign effect of Paris. The passage has a different beginning in each, and will illustrate the type of emendation that occurred as a consequence of the divorce of the Methuen manuscript from that of the Harper:

Methuen	*Harper and* *New York Edition*
With his letters in his lap then, in his Luxembourg nook—letters held with nervous, unconscious intensity— he thought of things in a strange, vast order, swinging at moments off into space, into past and future, and then dropping fast, with some loss of breath, but with a soft, reassuring thud, down to yesterday and to-day. Thus it was that he came back to his puzzle of the evening, the question of whether he could have taken Chad to such a play, and what effect —it was a point that suddenly rose —his responsibility in respect to Chad might be held to have, in general, on his choice of entertainment.	This suggested the question of whether he could properly have taken him to such a play, and what effect —it was a point that suddenly rose —his peculiar responsibility might be held to have, in general, [*New York Edition:* might be held in general to have] on his choice of entertainment.

It can be seen that James, in the Methuen edition, introduces a sentence providing transition from the preceding paragraph. The entire passage in question, which contains the image of Paris as a "vast bright Babylon" and "a jewel brilliant and hard," ends with a much more extensive interpolation in the Methuen:

Methuen	*Harper and* *New York Edition*
. . . the exchange again, as was fairly to be presumed, of the vaunted best French for something that might in a manner be a part of that ambiguous ideal, but was certainly not the part permitting publicity, either of appreciation or of discussion, in respect to varieties of quality.	. . . the exchange again, as was fairly to be presumed, of the vaunted best French for some special variety of the worst.

Immediately after this, James inserted in the Methuen edition the following sentences not in the other editions:

All Mrs. Newsome had now for a long time known of her son was that he had renewed his career in the expensive district—it was so, she felt, that she sufficiently designated it—and that he had not so established himself without intimate countenance. He had travelled, in the dreadful direction, almost like a Pasha—save that his palanquins had been by no means curtained and their occupants far from veiled; he had, in short, had company—scandalous, notorious company—across the bridges, company making with him, in the cynical journey, from stage to stage and from period to period, bolder pushes and taking larger freedoms: traces, echoes, almost legends, all these things, left in the wake of the pair.

The student of James's texts of *The Ambassadors,* it can be seen, must reckon with the Methuen edition as a separate entity.

The Harper text underwent a fairly attentive and careful though not strenuous revision in preparation for the New York Edition. Commas were struck out right and left, and stylistic changes were made to give the prose more fluidity. Thus, in the first paragraph of the misplaced chapter, James made two changes, in addition to deleting a number of commas; "have not" became "haven't" and the "easier chair" became the "easiest chair." But what we can imagine James as doing on this occasion—it was in 1908, with Scribner pressing him for copy—is revising in batches of pages without regard for chapter sequence. (What author, after all, would entertain a suspicion that his chapters were in the wrong order, once the book had been processed by a reputable publishing house?)

The chapter thus remained misplaced in the New York Edition. But since this was the edition that embodied James's ultimate revisions, it would seem to assert itself as the definitive text rather than the earlier and more prolix Methuen edition, which James assembled from a mixture of galleys and carbon sheets.

The misplaced chapter was discovered by Robert E. Young, a student of Yvor Winters, who published his finding in *American Litera-*

ture in 1950,[18] but failed to consult the important Methuen edition. Mr. Winters in a subsequent article developed Young's argument that James was a bad writer indeed if his chapter remained misplaced and unnoticed for half a century.[19] I would suggest that one could argue the reverse with greater validity—that there has been bad reading rather than bad writing (and of course careless publishing).

Four years after Young's article appeared, some of the textual discrepancies were independently reported by Susan M. Humphreys in *Notes and Queries.*[20] She did not notice, however, that an entire chapter was misplaced, but assumed James had been guilty of careless revision of his text for the New York Edition. On its discovery by Mr. Young, the error was drawn to the attention of Harper & Brothers, and in 1955 the firm announced that it would be corrected. In November 1958 the Harper news letter, *Harper Books and Authors,* disclosed, however, that copies had come back from the printer months before with the chapter misplaced again. It had finally been put into its proper place, the news letter announced, in November 1957.

Of the recent paperbacks, the Anchor edition, edited by R. W. Stallman, was advertised as restoring the chapters to proper order. Moreover, it was represented by the editor in his foreword as being a "faithful copy" of the Methuen edition. However, the edition that was published followed the erroneous Harper edition of 1903. Stallman went on to edit the Signet edition, where he reproduced the Methuen text and attributed to the publishers of Anchor the responsibility for their printing of the wrong text. The Fawcett edition reproduced the corrected Harper text of 1957. Riverside and Rinehart reproduce the New York Edition, but with restoration of the chapters to proper sequence.

[18] "An Error in *The Ambassadors,*" *American Literature,* XXII (1950), 245–53.
[19] "Problems for the Modern Critic of Literature," *Hudson Review,* IX (1956), 349–50.
[20] "Henry James's Revisions for 'The Ambassadors,'" *Notes and Queries,* n. s., I (1954), 397–99.

The Achieved Life à la Henry James

by Maxwell Geismar

It is curious how James displayed all the traits of the established "upper class" group of the older American republic confronted by the new power, the vulgarity, the materialism of the robber baron period. But also James *shared* certain values and tastes of the new American fortunes themselves; and in his last major novel of an aging "provincial" and European "culture," he revealed himself as perhaps the greatest provincial of them all in American literature. "Europe" —this yearned-for, imaginary identity of his youth—persisted forever and ever in an endless and untouchable dream of "art" and culture high above the mundane events of ordinary life. The same fantasy of James's childhood and adolescence, though now refurbished "for others" in *The Ambassadors,* persisted in his maturity and old age, and now in a heightened and even more fabricated form. "He's delightful; he's wonderful," both Miss Barrace and Little Bilham repeat in unison about the dour, uncomprehending, comic-opera "Yankee," Waymarsh, who is also not much removed from the small-town New England lawyer in *Roderick Hudson.* (Just as this whole Paris scene was a "retake," at best a "remake," of the glittering Roman scene in James's first novel, where the little Dickensian painter, Sam Singleton, and the "sophisticated" Miss Blanchard were the prototypes for Little Bilham and Miss Barrace.) Henry James was never one to be changed by experience. "Dear old Paris!" all these expatriated "artists" echo in their communal chorus, and: "She's charming; she's perfect . . . she's wonderful," they exclaim about Mme. de Vionnet herself. This was a kind of fairy-tale masque of Parisian life—of a glittering, marvelous, beautiful world of ambassadors and duchesses and artists—rather than any kind of realistic appraisal. But just as in *The Wings of the Dove,* or as in all the later James novels, there is an added layer of deception. They are all in the plot—this whole cast of cultivated European figures—

to deceive Strether (who hardly needs their help), to keep him in ignorance about the obvious relationship of Chad and Mme. de Vionnet.

Chad himself begins to hint ominously and mysteriously about "the damnable terms of my sacrifice," and how much he owes to Mme. de Vionnet. (She is beginning to age, she is almost forty. He has grown tired of her anyhow; he will not risk his American wealth and position for her sake.) In the novel there is hardly any direct view of Chad and Mme. de Vionnet together; they barely speak to each other in this "intimate" relationship. But meanwhile Strether has met her and he himself has fallen completely in love with her feminine charm, her culture (she subscribes to the *Revue de Deux Mondes*), her plight. It is Strether now, despite the risk of his own career and his intended marriage to Mrs. Newsome, who urges Chad to keep Mme. de Vionnet and to defy the puritanical American codes and conventions. "I understand what a relation with such a woman— what such a high fine friendship—may be. It can't be vulgar or coarse, anyway—and that's the point," he declares, and then: "Let them face the future together." And here, at the close of the first volume, *The Ambassadors*, in its own odd way, despite all the implausible nonsense of its background, and perhaps the even more dubious nature of its "plot," does achieve a certain tension, sympathy and interest.

That is the familiar "secret" of the Jamesian literary magic; of making the unreal, or the half real, seem real for the moment as we read the novel, at least; or if not quite "real," at least "convincing," or if not quite convincing, somehow and someway interesting. This is the special Jamesian "illusion" of literature and life, again, spreading its own wings of artifice over our infatuated fancies; even though so obviously based on such a transparent web of "magic yearning" and wishful thinking. Mme. de Vionnet, worried and anxious about Chad and his American family, persuades Strether to help her case, just when the handsome young pagan is preparing to leave her; and to pay her off. Strether clearly faces the "truth"—"as with dormant pulses at last awake"—and stakes everything on his own belief. He concedes that Bilham, the poor little painter-man, is not good enough for Mme. de Vionnet's cultivated daughter, Jeanne, who has been the previous blind for Chad's "interest" in the French household.

There are curious psychological elements, of course, in the central relationships of the novel. Earlier Chad is almost viewed as a paternal figure seeking the hand of his mistress's daughter. Now Strether, in his own passion and enthusiasm, takes over the role of the father-surrogate who is persuading an unruly "son" to keep an aging mistress-mother symbol—a "pure" father-figure on Strether's part, but one who is also in love with the woman with whom the son is obviously on the most intimate terms. These shadowy and shifting familial and filial relations, centered around an unconscious or repressed incestuous triangle, accompanied, very often, by a sublimated homosexual or lesbian situation, are evident in James's work as far back as *The Bostonians* or *Watch and Ward.* They were even more explicitly developed in the novel which followed *The Ambassadors*—despite all the Jamesian critics who stressed his rational and conscious, or moral and metaphysical grandeur. How often indeed did the later James, increasingly obsessed by "sex," play so delicately with these "abnormal," or historically "primitive," or infantile states of the human psyche—and perhaps that, too, is almost unconsciously part of our concern with the Chad-Strether-Vionnet triangle in the novel.

One notes, incidentally, that Mme. de Vionnet's daughter Jeanne —but not Chad's—is cast in the familiar role of the child-orphan exploited by the callous adults. For Mme. de Vionnet forces her into a "suitable marriage"; partly, we are told, because Chad *has* had his eye on her, and also because Madame wishes to free herself entirely of any encumbrances Chad might object to. So not only is the attachment between Strether and the charming French lady—sentimental and romantic as it is—another "impossible" love affair of James's; but Mme. de Vionnet's charm itself soon becomes questionable, and her character dubious. Here as in *The Wings of the Dove*, after the brief interlude of Jamesian enchantment, the central figures of the novel are soon transfixed by their "prearranged destinies." They are trapped again by the relentless coils of the romance melodrama. In one sense indeed the three main figures can be viewed as an aging, desperate and manipulative woman; a rich, slippery and callous young American bounder; and a perpetually adolescent, rather pruriently old-maidish and inordinately "innocent" middle-aged voyeur. For Strether also "spies out," with a kind of childish wonder, and a certain curious loverlike jealousy and envy, all the "intimate" sexual behavior of Chad and Mme. de Vionnet. In a more realistic chronicle, this after all barely more than middle-aged literary man, completely entranced as he is by the maturing French lady, might well have married her. And the well-matched couple might then have left their wealthy, handsome, cultivated and "pagan" young American friend to go his own idle way.

But this is impossible, of course, in the typical Jamesian view of reality, human behavior, or experience. It is much too sensible, possible and practical. If Mme. de Vionnet is "strange and beautiful" to Strether in "her quiet soft acuteness," we are shortly told that "the golden nail she had driven in pierced a good inch deeper." If Chad is "strong and sleek and gay, easy and fragrant and fathomless," he becomes all the more ambiguous about his future plans when Strether becomes more importunate. "Are you tired of her?" asks the infatuated intermediary of this odd triangle:

> Chad gave him in reply to this, with a movement of the head, the strangest slow smile he had ever had from him.
> "Never."
> "Never?"
> "Never?" asks Strether again.

And: "Never," says Chad, "obligingly and serenely," in this typical later-James verbal interchange. But he is, of course. And he has already decided to leave her. Then there is the celebrated arrival of the Pococks in the novel (as the Jacobites proclaim) as the real emissaries of the vigilant, rich, powerful, threatening, puritanical and provincial (if always absent) New England mother-figure, Mrs. Newsome herself.

Yes, they do provide a kind of familiar and accomplished light-comedy touch in *The Ambassadors*. But Sarah Pocock also—with "her marked thin-lipped smile, intense without brightness and as prompt to act as the scrape of a safety-match," and "the protrusion of her rather remarkably long chin," and "the penetration of her voice to a distance," is the Jamesian stereotype of the angular, virginal, narrow and chill New England woman. Beneath the entertainment, Henry James's animus towards this area of American life was as persistent as his view of New England was fixed. As for Jim Pocock himself—

> Small and fat and constantly facetious, straw-coloured and destitute of marks, he would have been practically indistinguishable hadn't his constant preference for light-grey clothes, for white hats, for very big cigars and very little stories, done what it could for his identity.

—he is another caricature of the American businessman: a pre-Babbitt or pre-Dodsworth figure, also in Edith Wharton's vein, who comes off less harshly perhaps because he is after all the victim and puppet of the dominating New England women. Less harshly, but not too convincingly, because *as* an American businessman there is nothing in him of the business world except an incurable, gaping tourist-type misunderstanding of "Europe."

What is curious, however, in the novel's big confrontation scene of Europe and America—of the Pococks and Mme. de Vionnet; where Strether finally declares himself as Europe's friend—is that neither side of this rather forced, artificial ideological debate comes out very well. If the Americans are stupid and vulgar, Mme. de Vionnet is

obviously scheming, self-pitying and rather tactless. From this point
on her character falls apart rapidly—the moves in "her game" become
apparent. "Do I seem to you very awful?" she asks Strether; and even
with the advantage of her "noble old apartment" which is "full, once
more, of dim historic shades, of the faint far-away cannon-roar of the
great empire," Mme. de Vionnet becomes, if not "awful," at least a
selfish or even a stupid woman. And when this heroine collapses,
the novel collapses. We suddenly become aware of the celebrated
"method" of the narrative: the indirect presentation through a series
of alternating conversations; the different points of view always centered around the meaning of the events rather than of personality;
the "pre-anterior" analysis of events to come, the anterior analysis,
the event itself, and then the series of "post-analyses." But we become
aware of this intricate, elaborate and artificial method simply because
the novel's content has ebbed away. In the "circular narrative" which
constitutes the form of *The Ambassadors*—this "architectural roundness" which James considered to be at its height and perfection here
—it is quite possible to omit several rings of the exposition without
doing much harm to the story's meaning. These are really duplicating
interpretations, or what one might call also "the skippable exposition." (Thus the famous "reversed" chapters, which are not really
reversed at all.)

How far was James deliberate or unconscious, again, in charting
Mme. de Vionnet's disintegration? Was this a measure of Strether's
dawning European consciousness, his so-long-delayed social maturity?
Was it also a necessary attribute of the plot line, in order to rationalize
Chad's desertion of her, to make him a little less of a cad? There
was still another, deeper, typically Jamesian reason, perhaps. In a
climactic scene towards the novel's end, when Strether, too, abandons
Mme. de Vionnet—for no reason that you can see, except that perhaps
he has finally discovered, with a pang of jealousy and a blush of
shame, "the deep, deep truth of the intimacy revealed"—with Chad,
that is; and when James again invoked the glorious French past, not
of the grand empire but this time of the Revolution itself to serve
as the dying chord of his doomed heroine—

> Thus and so, on the eve of the great recorded dates, the days and
> nights of revolution, the sounds had come in, the omens, the begin-
> nings broken out. They were the smell of revolution, the smell of the
> public temper—or perhaps simply the smell of blood . . . His hostess
> was dressed as for thunderous times, and it fell in with the kind of
> imagination we have just attributed to him that she should be in the
> simplest coolest white, of a character so old-fashioned, if he were not

mistaken, that Madame Roland must on the scaffold have worn something like it . . .

—in this dramatic or even somewhat melodramatic scene of Mme. de
Vionnet's final ruin, we may come across the real reason for her
decline.

James again stressed her "cultural value," her connections with an
"old, old, old" race and tradition; her association with "things from
far back—tyrannies of history, facts of type, values, as the painters
said, of expression—all working for her and giving her the supreme
chance, the chance of the happy, the really luxurious few . . ."
And the Jacobite critics of *The Ambassadors* make much of the fact
that here, somewhat as in *The Princess Casamassima*, this artist used
the great moments of French history to add "tradition," "depth,"
"tone" to his condemned heroine. But consider for a moment just
what view of French history James adduced in these passages of romantic rhetoric about the "grand Empire," the Revolutionary Terror,
and Mme. Roland on the scaffold. After all, was it so unusual in
French society for a wealthy young man to discard an older mistress?
Did this really warrant the "smell of the public temper," which was
equated, in this Jamesian "history," with the smell of blood?

No; all this was simply another dubious and metaphysical smoke
screen of Henry James's, another adolescent-romantic "picture" of
French history and culture as embodied in the doomed Mme. de
Vionnet. And this heroine was not as "natural and simple" with the
grandeur of condemned royalty as James here described her—as James
himself then grudgingly admitted. Strether could "trust her," as we
are told; but: "That is he could trust her to make deception right.
As she presented things the ugliness—goodness knows why—went
out of them; none the less too that she could present them, with
an art of her own, by not as much as touching them."

But then what *was* this "deception," this "ugliness" and this art
of omission which is also embodied in Mme. de Vionnet? For James
finally did reach—after all the elaborate "counter-screens" so to speak,
of her charm, tact, beauty, culture, art, simplicity—the flaw in Mme.
de Vionnet. "Women were thus endlessly absorbent, and to deal with
them was to walk on water," Strether reflects in an illuminating
phrase:

> What was at bottom the matter with her, embroider as she might and
> disclaim as she might [or as James might]—what was at bottom the matter
> with her was simply Chad himself. It was of Chad she was after all
> renewedly afraid; the strange strength of her passion was the very strength
> of her fear; she clung to *him*, Lambert Strether, as to a source of safety

she had tested, and, generous, graceful, truthful as she might try to be, exquisite as she was, she dreaded the term of his being within reach. With this sharpest perception yet, it was like a chill in the air to him, it was almost appalling, that a creature so fine could be, by mysterious forces, a creature so exploited.

And Strether finally tells Mme. de Vionnet: "You're afraid for your life!"

Now there is a certain truth in all this eloquence with which James recurrently propounded his own deepest fear and suspicion of the "passions." They do indeed exact their toll—the hard vow of the goddess—upon their deluded and inflamed victims; they do exploit the finest creatures impaled upon these "mysterious forces"; while fear, anxiety, deception are their psychological concomitants, as the bards, the poets and the novelists of love have always told us. But is this the single medium of the passions? Is it love's *only* conclusion; its only premise and only reward—and was this Mme. de Vionnet's only true moment of revelation and sincerity in *The Ambassadors?* What was illuminating in this Jamesian passage was the deep tone of horror with which it regarded love and passion as the destructive agent of all human grace, dignity, and even beauty.

It was actually moreover as if he didn't think of her at all, as if he could think of nothing but the passion, mature, abysmal, pitiful, she represented and the possibilities she betrayed. She was older for him to-night, visibly less exempt from the touch of time; but was as much as ever the finest and subtlest creature, the happiest apparition, it had been given to him, in all his years, to meet; and yet he could see her there as vulgarly troubled, in very truth, as a maidservant crying for her young man. The only thing was that she judged herself as the maidservant wouldn't; the weakness of which wisdom, too, the dishonour of which judgment seemed but to sink her lower.

So now the secret was out. The Jamesian half-truth about the passions in the heroine of *The Ambassadors* was the same, familiar fixed fantasy in the Jamesian mind as to not only the destructive impact of passion, but its final cheapness and vulgarity. Mme. de Vionnet was the highest product of French culture, as James implied, whose whole merit was that she has reclaimed and re-educated the brash, provincial young American millionaire, whose whole mysterious sexuality has been employed, as it were, for a purely cultural and "social" purpose. But Mme. de Vionnet is punished in the novel because, after all, she *is* sexual. Or else why did James describe her passion as "mature, abysmal, pitiful"? And what "possibilities" has Mme. de Vionnet betrayed? Why is she suddenly so much older, and as "vulgarly troubled" in truth, as the Jamesian maidservant crying for her young man? (Like the prurient Victorians in general, James apparently identified the "lower passions" with the lower classes; or sometimes even, as we see in the literature of this period, with "the lower races.") And was James so certain that a maidservant *wouldn't* judge herself—about what?—while Mme. de Vionnet's self-image now revealed only the weakness of her wisdom, the dishonor and depths of her shame?

If the handsome villainess in *The Wings of the Dove* showed that sexuality was at base criminal, the enchanting, subtle and cultivated heroine of *The Ambassadors* showed that sex was still disastrous— even when there was a minimum of it in this "virtuous" alliance; and when that minimum was used, in the Jamesian view, for the noblest of social purposes. Now this whole tragedy of Mme. de Vionnet's "ruin" simply reflected, in a somewhat less obvious way, the abiding Jamesian superstition that sexual love, just as in the phobic fantasies of *The Sacred Fount,* was not a source of life and pleasure, but was a hideous, devouring and destructive process. Mme. de Vionnet is ruined, after all, because she has made Chad what he is. (She is a literary cousin of May Server, of May Bartram.) She has given everything to him; he has taken it all without qualms and without reciprocity; and all that is left for this heroine is abysmal and vulgar grief. Strether abandons her in her deepest moment of need; though why? Chad abandons her without even a farewell recorded in the novel. And the two men have a final, quite euphoric (and illogical) post-mortem on this suffering woman. "She must have been wonderful," says Strether. "She *was*," says the young American mercantile prince.

But was she, really? The great Jamesian buildup of Mme. de Vionnet's charm, grace, beauty, tact, wisdom now appears again merely to be contrived, forced and strained in the light of its true purpose in the novel, and the Jamesian moral she illustrates. Her portrait is an- other technical "counter-screen" in large part, designed to hide her real meaning until the very end; and hence the adolescent and exaggerated view of her charm on the part of Strether—the contrived view by James himself. And thus we get those almost always enigmatic "glimpses" of Mme. de Vionnet, the reflections and refractions of her "charm"—and the one famous scene of her sitting in the rowboat with her lover; the "glimpse" indeed that condemns her—since to approach too closely to her character before the close of *The Ambassadors* would give the whole thing away. But then James never could ap- proach any of his charming heroines too closely. It was his technical virtuosity that could create this "charm" on such an insubstantial base of knowledge, on such a partial innocent and fearful view of women in general.

If you remember Mme. de Vionnet's peers in the American literature of the period—the lovely, graceful and mature Mme. Olenska of Edith Wharton's fiction, for example; or even the practical, simple little Sister Carrie of Dreiser's—the Jamesian heroine is attractive, yes, but inadequate. She is inadequate precisely because she is attractive—and so unfulfilled as a woman even within her own terms. The final "revelation" of her plight also marks the wind-up of Strether's own career, entranced as he has been by this "happy apparition" of ancient French femininity. But what, after all, *was* his career? The novel ends with a familiar series of rather touching Jamesian "farewells"—to Strether, to Chad, to Maria Gostrey, whom Strether might also have married, in a more realistic chronicle, if Mme. de Vionnet had become out of the question. But this middle-aged "observer," still living out his life through all these other people, prefers to dwell alone with his new European sensibility. That is the only human gain in the novel, apparently; that is the familiar Jamesian "moral."

Is it enough, even for a lighter novel of social comedy on the international theme? Well, here as in *The Wings of the Dove*, the real base is that of solid cash. "Shall you give up your friend for the money in it?" Strether finally asks Chad directly, while the handsome young American pagan has become immersed, conveniently, in his new theories of "scientific advertising." As for Strether's own "ruin," he is not averse to renouncing the wealthy, dominating, puritanical American widow, Mrs. Newsome. He still has "a little money" of his own, while Chad assures him fervently that "he mustn't starve." That is what lingers with us, curiously, after we have finished reading *The Ambassadors,* interesting and entertaining as it is in parts—if also quite pretentious, overblown and tedious in other sections of its extended "analyses" of such meager content. Otherwise, after the spell of James's own literary magic has subsided—the magic-magic of illusion, artifice and pretense—we may wonder just what *is* in the novel, beyond the endless chatter of a group of fashionable expatriates and mediocrities, dwelling in an obviously inadequate and patently artificial "international scene."

What an esoteric fiction, in short, this was; and how James could still blow it up to such inordinate proportions. Perhaps his real gift lay in the immense fertility of trivia with which we are constantly beguiled under the pretense of importance. If *The Ambassadors* is at least highly readable (when it is readable at all), how thin, forced and superficial it appears upon any real reflection or analysis. (In this respect it anticipates J. P. Marquand's later blend of "romance" and innocuous social satire; perhaps Henry James helped to fashion that attractive but inconsequential literary genre.) This novel is probably the most ingenious of all the Jamesian "games of art," and the novel which is most clearly just a game. That is possibly the reason why the contemporary Jacobites, who followed James's dictum and Matthiessen's solemn explication that this was quite the best, "all round," of the later novels, have found it so difficult to make any case for their claim.

It is a false claim, and there is no case. Almost all "pre-action" and "post-post-analysis," the human content of *The Ambassadors* is limited; the view of human behavior is dubious; the moral is particularly Jamesian and arbitrary; the literary method is exotic, orotund and verbose. All that remains is a sentimental romance, an entertaining fiction in parts, which has a certain charm at the expense of credibility.

"O Rare for Strether!" *Antony and Cleopatra*

and *The Ambassadors*

by U. C. Knoepflmacher

> *Cleopatra.* I'll seem the fool I am not. Antony
> Will be himself.
> *Antony.*   But stirred by Cleopatra.
> Now for the love of Love and her soft hours,
> Let's not confound the time with conference
> harsh.
> There's not a minute of our lives should stretch
> Without some pleasure now. What sport tonight?
> *Cleopatra.* Hear the ambassadors.[1]

> This place and these impressions of Chad and of people I've
> seen at *his* place—well, have had their abundant message for
> me. . . . I see it now. I haven't done so enough before—and
> now I'm old; too old at any rate for what I see. Oh, I *do* see,
> at least; and more than you'd believe or I can express . . . the
> right time now is yours. The right time is *any* time that one
> is still so lucky as to have. . . . Of course I don't take you for
> a fool, or I shouldn't be addressing you thus awfully. . . .
> Live! [2]

Students of *The Ambassadors* have inevitably approached the novel
through the central figure of Lewis Lambert Strether and, after the
manner of Percy Lubbock, have treated him as a "worn, intelligent,
clear-sighted man." [3] Although some critics have disputed the clarity
of Strether's vision,[4] it is still customary to endow James's protagonist

---

[1] *Antony and Cleopatra*, I, i, 44–48.

[2] Henry James, *The Ambassadors* (New York, Doubleday Anchor Books, 1958),
pp. 163–64. Future references in the text are to this edition.

[3] *The Craft of Fiction* (New York, n.d. [1922?]), p. 168.

with a "superior sensibility" which gives him "a capacity to live." [5] Indeed, the novel as a whole is usually regarded as a depiction of Strether's belated education in "life": "it is Strether himself and not Chad, who has, during these amazing six months, lived." [6] Strether's speech to little Bilham in Gloriani's garden is taken as evidence for his reawakened "sense of life"; his failure as Mrs. Newsome's ambassador is regarded as a pyrrhic victory, but a victory after all; his delusions about Chad and Mme. de Vionnet are mitigated by references to his idealism and to the "positive suffering" and "tragic French passion" that he learns from that lady's example.[7] Mme. de Vionnet's last encounter with Strether in chapter xxxiii of the novel thus conveys a lesson in "humanity" through which Strether presumably achieves the final "expansion of his social and moral awareness," an awareness which causes him to reject nobly the worlds of Paris and of America.[8]

A recent critic, Robert E. Garis, opposes this standard reading of the novel and argues firmly that, instead, "there has been no education at all." [9] Strether's quickened sense of life collapses as he discovers that he has been totally unable to cope with the European realities he has repeatedly professed to "see" and to understand. The final confrontation between the American and Mme. de Vionnet only confirms the extent of his defeat, when Strether tries to fuse the moral disgust and romantic admiration that he feels for his young friend's mistress by mentally transforming her grief for the imminent loss of her young lover into Cleopatra's regal bereavement over the aged Antony's death.[10] There is a curious blend of incongruities in Strether's abstraction:

> She was older for him to-night, visibly less exempt from the touch of time; but she was as much as ever the finest and noblest creature, the

---

[4] See, for instance, Quentin Anderson, *The American Henry James* (New Brunswick, New Jersey, 1957), pp. 211ff., and Robert E. Garis, "The Two Lambert Strethers: A New Reading of *The Ambassadors*," *MFS*, VII (Winter 1961–62), 305–16.

[5] Oscar Cargill, *The Novels of Henry James* (New York, 1961), p. 328.

[6] Stephen Spender, *The Destructive Element* (Philadephia, 1953), p. 79. See also F. O. Matthiessen, *Henry James* (New York, 1944), pp. 30–41; F. W. Dupee, *Henry James* (New York, 1956), pp. 207–15; Frederick C. Crews, *The Tragedy of Manners* (New Haven, Connecticut, 1957), pp. 35–56.

[7] Matthiessen, p. 41; Dupee, p. 215.

[8] Crews, pp. 54, 55.

[9] Garis, p. 309.

[10] The allusion, as Garis points out, is an ironic echo of *Antony and Cleopatra*, IV, xv, 73–75, in which the grieving Cleopatra addresses Charmian and Iras and professes to be "No more but e'en a woman, and commanded / By such poor passion as the maid that milks / And does the meanest chores."

happiest apparition, it had been given to him in all his years, to meet;
and yet he could see her there as vulgarly troubled, in very truth, as
a maidservant crying for her young man (p. 435).

Strether's conflicting feelings have sought a sufficiently ambivalent
vehicle in Cleopatra, a "queen" and a "quean." But his attempted
fusion is a failure. The nobility of this "apparition" becomes subverted
by Strether's sense of her vulgarity; the timeless creature concocted by
his imagination stands before him as an aging *femme du monde*.
Strether's idealization cannot sustain him. He is vanquished by the
extremes of "life," by Paris and by America.

While I agree with Garis's reading of this scene and with his
over-all interpretation of the novel, I cannot accept the basic assumption on which he builds his argument, namely, that James's introduction of Strether's defeat constitutes a complete reversal of his initial
purpose; that, for some inexplicable reason, the author suddenly
altered the conception of his protagonist; and that, as a consequence,
"the last seven chapters [xxx to xxxvi] turn against and annihilate the
earlier ones." [11] In the section which follows I shall try to show that,
quite to the contrary, the confrontation scene in chapter xxxiii is the
culmination of a carefully constructed sequence, begun early in the
novel, which depicts Strether's progressive abstraction of Chad's mistress into Shakespeare's Cleopatra, an abstraction made even more
ironic by his resulting, unconsciously wishful, self-portrayal as the
Antony of his imagined queen.

Strether's play acting informs the novel's meaning. Like his Shakespearean prototype, Strether hovers between two hostile worlds, a
world of strict codes and observances and a world of amorality and
laxity. Like Antony, he is seduced by the rarified atmosphere of the
older of these two worlds; like Antony, he sees, or professes to see, a
"life" he has ignored in his youth, hoping to "stretch" its pleasures
through his reawakened imagination; like Antony, Strether is ultimately betrayed both by his fancy and by his fancied queen. But
Antony acts upon his vision, and his defeat is a triumph which is
denied to his American counterpart. For Shakespeare's hero translates
imagination into action; he bequeathes his imagination to his queen,
stimulates her sacrifice, and, through it, transcends his own ignoble
death by becoming a giant "past the size of dreaming." Through
Cleopatra, "such a man as this" has become a possibility: "Nature
wants stuff to vie strange forms with fancy." Whereas Antony is thus
able to "stretch," Strether is not. His imagination, vicarious and power-

[11] Garis, p. 305.

less, relies solely on the attachments of others and falls outside the realm of will and action.[12] Strether can only contract reality into preconceived forms: "one 'takes' the form," he tells little Bilham, "and is more or less compactly held by it" (p. 163).

I

Strether's abstraction of Mme. de Vionnet into an imaginary Cleopatra is the product of "those frequent phenomena of mental reference with which all judgment in him was actually beset" (p. 105). His first vision of the aristocratic lady among the relics of old Paris fires the starved imagination that has been rekindled since his landing in England.[13] In chapter xiii, Strether meets Mme. de Vionnet. So far, he has imagined "horrors." He has asked, with hesitating candor, whether Chad is "—what shall I say?—monstrous" (p. 100). But now the sight of the lady herself assuages his misgivings, for she becomes qualified by the associations suggested by her surroundings, the remnants of a romantic world "he vaguely thought of as the world of Chateaubriand, of Mme. de Staël, of the young Lamartine" (p. 184). As Strether looks at Mme. de Vionnet, he finds himself subjected to a curious emotional process:

> At the back of his head, behind everything, was the sense that she was —there, before him, close to him, in vivid, imperative form—one of the rare women he had so often heard of, read of, thought of, but never met, whose very presence, look, voice, the mere contemporaneous *fact* of

[12] Professor Cargill feels that Strether commits himself to a "decisive action" in his final interview with Mme. de Vionnet (p. 315). If so, Strether's "action," a hasty retreat, is certainly thrust upon him by circumstances. The Antony-Strether and Cleopatra–Mme. de Vionnet parallels (Professor Cargill dismisses the latter as having no more than a "momentary pertinence" [p. 327]) provide a mock-heroic frame of reference which only accentuates Strether's inaction and indecisiveness.

[13] The editor of the "green" Woollett Literary Review can cope with the European reality only by cross-references to his bookish knowledge of its literature and art. His own name, "Lewis Lambert," is, as Maria Gostrey reminds him, taken from the title of an "awfully bad" novel by Balzac (p. 11). Maria herself recalls for Strether the image of "Major Pendennis breakfasting at his club" (p. 26). He regards the sculptor Gloriani as a "dazzling prodigy of type" only because he knows that the "work of his hand" is admired (p. 147). Strether's excitement to find Mme. de Vionnet at Notre Dame, later in the novel, is heightened for him by his previous purchase of the works of Victor Hugo in "seventy bound volumes, a miracle of cheapness" (p. 222). Strether has obviously forgotten his earlier, unsuccessful attempt to raise a "temple of taste" for himself and his wife on the foundation of a European hoard of "lemon-colored volumes" which soon became "stale and soiled" (p. 65).

whom, from the moment it was all presented, made a relation of mere recognition. That was not the kind of woman he had ever found Mrs. Newsome, a contemporaneous fact who had been distinctly slow to establish herself; and at present, confronted with Mme. de Vionnet, he felt the simplicity of his original impression of Miss Gostrey (pp. 189–90).

Strether's conversion is instantaneous. His "impression" of Mme. de Vionnet is totally unlike those that he has had of Mrs. Newsome, Maria Gostrey, and, one can safely assume, of his deceased American wife.[14] The lovely Frenchwoman facing him is refracted into an imaginary figure, "an imperative form" which demands his immediate submission. But this submission is purely mental and therefore proper and decorous. Strether yields not to the physical reality before him but to his own wishful abstraction of it. At the conclusion of the chapter, he promises with the candid devotion of the love-servant of some legendary *court d'amour,* "I'll save you if I can" (p. 192).

But Strether's imagination has not yet found the proper correlative for the "rare woman" he has seen. Mme. de Vionnet is, after all, a *femme du monde,* and the New Englander's "feeling" for this "category" has at best been "light, romantic and mysterious" (p. 150). He needs a more adequate "form" to hold his imagination. It is the lively Miss Barrace who, of all people, provides Strether with the appropriate image for his sentimentalization. In chapter xiv, the little lady offers an explanation for the "charm" and "mood" which Strether finds so indescribable: "She's various. She's fifty women" (p. 199). Strether is satisfied. He is dazzled by the sight of the approaching Mme. de Vionnet, who makes her entrance just after he has gaily conceded that the lady's attachment to Chad must indeed be "an innocent one" and has laughingly deprecated his own attachment to Maria Gostrey. Stimulated by Miss Barrace's suggestion, Strether has now found the literary prototype demanded by his imagination. For the vision of Mme. de Vionnet confirms her "variety." Thus, chapter xv opens with Strether's mental portrayal of Mme. de Vionnet as Shakespeare's infinitely various queen. The description which begins in the second sentence clearly evokes Enobarbus' famous characterization of the apparition that sailed into Antony's view "upon the river Cydnus" (II, ii, 191–219). Yet, characteristically enough, the sensual description soon gives way to Strether's fanciful escape from the "contemporaneous fact" before him:

---

[14] Strether, James implies, loved his wife best after her death, "so insanely [giving] himself to merely missing the mother" that he "stupidly sacrificed" her son (p. 63). Life and the living are denied by abstraction. Antony's reaction to the death of his first wife, Fulvia, seems relevant: "What our contempts doth often hurl from us, / We wish it ours again" (I, ii, 119–20).

She had struck our friend, from the first of her appearing, as dressed for a great occasion, and she met still more than on either of the others the conception reawakened in him at their garden party, the idea of the *femme du monde* in her habit as she lived. Her bare shoulders and arms were white and beautiful; the materials of her dress, a mixture, as he supposed, of silk and crape, were of a silvery grey so artfully composed as to give an impression of warm splendor; and round her neck she wore a collar of large old emeralds, the green note of which was more dimly repeated, at other points of her apparel, in embroidery, in enamel, in satin, in substances and textures vaguely rich. Her head, extremely fair and exquisitely festal, was like a happy fancy, a notion of the antique, on an old, precious medal, some silver coin of the Renaissance; while her slim lightness and brightness, her gayety, her expression, her decision, contributed to an effect that might have been felt by a poet as half mythological and half conventional. He could have compared her to a goddess still partly engaged in a morning cloud, or to a sea-nymph waist-high in the summer surge. Above all she suggested to him the reflection that the *femme du monde*—was, like Cleopatra in the play, indeed various and multifold (p. 204).

The irony of the passage is obvious. Unlike Shakespeare, who could portray a "happy fancy" of antiquity on "some silver coin of the Renaissance," Strether's attempt to mythologize a *femme du monde* into a half-goddess is destined to become a mere counterfeit. Like Antony, Strether will have to pay "his heart for what his eyes eat only." [15]

Strether faithfully adheres to the imaginary portrait he now believes to have completed. Excitedly, he conducts his Cleopatra to a make-shift Nile, "the shining, barge-burdened Seine" (p. 226). He turns against his former allies and battles the new set of ambassadors sent by Woollett. He alienates the gruff but loyal Waymarsh; he finds his relationship with Maria Gostrey curiously altered. The accusing stare of Sarah Pocock disheartens him for a while, but he is emboldened by the presence of his make-believe queen:

Strether noticed her card on the table—her coronet and her "Comtesse" —and the imagination was sharp in him of certain private adjustments in Sarah's mind. She had never, he was sure, sat with a "Comtesse" before, and such was the specimen of that class he had been keeping to play on her (p. 285).

[15] In the simplistic view of Leslie A. Fiedler (*Love and Death in the American Novel* [New York, 1960]), it is of course not Strether but "James himself" who converts Mme. de Vionnet into a sea-nymph in order to conceal prudishly that "part of her anatomy the poetic cloud conventionally veils" (p. 293). Unclouded by such conventions, Fiedler modestly thanks his "own experience" for letting him know "what lies below the waist of Madame de Vionnet . . . for James is reluctant to make explicit the genital facts of the case" (p. 294).

Ironically enough, it is not Strether, but his trump Queen of Hearts, who is doing the playing and who seems to take the trick. Strether feels the "bravery" of Mme. de Vionnet's foray into the enemy camp. Imperceptibly and almost involuntarily, he finds himself drawn "into her boat" (p. 286), despite the implications immediately drawn by Waymarsh and Sarah Pocock:

> He recognized once more the perverse law that so inveterately governed his poor personal aspects: it would be certainly *like* the way things always turned out for him that he should affect Mrs. Pocock and Waymarsh as launched in a relation in which he had really never been launched at all. . . . But the flicker of fear on this occasion was not, as may be added, to repeat itself; it sprang up, for its moment, only to die down and then go forever. To meet his fellow-visitor's invocation and, with Sarah's brilliant eyes on him, answer, *was* quite sufficiently to step into her boat. During the rest of the time her visit lasted he felt himself proceed to each of the proper offices, successively, for helping to keep the adventurous skiff afloat. It rocked beneath him, but he settled in his place. He took up an oar, and since he was to have the credit of pulling, he pulled (p. 286).

Mme. de Vionnet has lulled Strether into acquiescence and converted him into an inert, but willing, ally who soon becomes conscious only of "the movement of the vessel itself" (p. 299). His "feet," he concludes with relief, are "firm," and, as always, he now feels that "he really did see" (pp. 306, 313). But it is Strether's Cleopatra of course, like Antony's, who controls the "adventurous skiff" and who becomes the instrument of his defeat. Strether's heart is tied to the rudder of his queen: his reversal comes by water.

The river scene in chapter xxxi corrects Strether's earlier vision. The portrait he has drawn is *not* complete. "A man who held the paddles and a lady, at the stern, with a pink parasol" drift into sight; it is Chad who "had been wanted in the picture" all along (p. 411). The image mocks Strether's previous sentimentalizations. Mme. de Vionnet is not a lovely Venus drifting into his sight on a golden barge, nor does this apparition invite *him* to pull the oars. Instead, Marie de Vionnet is what she has been all along, a *femme du monde,* now on a weekend tryst with her young lover. It is for this Cleopatra that Strether has defied the wrath of the Roman bride of Woollett, Mass.; it is because of her that he has been betrayed by Waymarsh, the blunt Enobarbus of Milrose; it is through her that he has idealized Chad into an ennobled and "living" younger counterpart of himself, a wishful substitute for the "dull" son he lost and never could accept.[16]

---

[16] Strether's relation to Waymarsh and Chad also recalls that of Antony to Ventidius and Dolabella in Dryden's *All For Love.* It is Ventidius who smuggles a new set of "ambassadors" into the temple of Isis in order to detach his friend

Paradoxically enough, Chad *is* Strether's counterpart, and the river scene serves to remind the older man that his vicarious play acting has been faulty and must come to a stop. Unable to relegate Chad into a secondary role, that of Jeanne de Vionnet's fiancé, afraid to probe into the true relationship between his Cleopatra and the young man, Strether's idealization of the pair had allowed him to step into the relationship itself, to settle into his queen's "skiff" with feet which were firm and dry. He had rendered Chad inoffensive and had thus been able to appropriate the role of Antony for himself. Now, "the right thing—a boat advancing round the bend" (p. 411) replaces Cleopatra's skiff and with it the displaced "Antony" reclaims his role. Strether must again become one of those "poor people who watch the play from the pit" (p. 393). The "right thing" mocks the idealization. Chad's careful precautions echo Strether's equally diligent search for a private "atmosphere" in which he could enjoy his Cleopatra to his full mental satisfaction—the secluded restaurant by "the barge-burdened Seine." But Chad, unlike Strether, seeks privacy for the "real thing." The impact is painful: "To the young Roman boy she hath sold me, and I fall / Under this plot: she dies for't. Eros, ho!" (IV, xii, 48–49). Shakespeare's Antony does not carry out his threat; he is the one to die as victim of his Egyptian serpent. James's Antony is equally impotent. His final confrontation with his Cleopatra also depicts a death of sorts.

Again, Strether submits to "the associations of the place"; again, he searches for "the noble analogy" that has sustained him in the past (p. 427). But he can no longer be "held" by the form. The reality he has consistently evaded now fails him in turn. "Visibly less exempt from the touch of time," Mme. de Vionnet reveals herself to her would-be Antony as a Cleopatra staled by custom and withered by age. She is a mere woman "afraid for [her] life," not a tragic heroine breathing passionate defiance (p. 435). "I'm old and abject and hideous," she complains rather querulously (p. 436). But it is Strether, and not she, who has shrivelled. For he has become aware that the woman standing before him is his creation and that not only she, but "he, a little," had made Chad seem far more "infinite" than he actually was (p. 434). Invoking the image of the bereaved Cleopatra, Strether can find only a vulgar maid-servant crying for her young man. The dead Antony could transform his Cleopatra's "poor passion" into a transcending power which resurrects him and raises him up "dolphin-like" into a colossus who straddles the ocean that separates two worlds. Strether is incapable of such a feat. He merely deplores his

---

from Cleopatra; it is Antony's jealousy of the young Dolabella which produces his eventual downfall.

drowning: "it took women, it took women; if to deal with them was to walk on water, what wonder that the water rose?" (p. 434).

Having furtively endowed Mme. de Vionnet with the sublimity that Antony openly bestowed upon his queen, Strether now avoids paying his predecessor's price, but, in doing so, he deprives himself also of the Roman's reward. For Strether has refused to become an active participant in life. He has preferred instead the safely decorous role of "ambassador," the messenger or go-between so mercilessly ridiculed and contemptuously treated by the Cleopatra of the play. His idealizations are shattered, not only because he discovers the vulgarity that taints his queen, but also because he realizes for the first time that he, Strether, could have been her Antony all along. She has "wanted" him, she tells him, suggesting at the same time, however, that she has wanted him in a sphere where the imagination must "get on" with "the appearances you've had to see" (pp. 436–37). This sphere, the sphere of life itself, is not for Strether. His reaction is a hasty retreat. His final words to his fancied queen are eloquent: "Ah, but you've *had* me!" (p. 437).

II

James's subtle exploitation of *Antony and Cleopatra* demonstrates the uniformity of his characterization of Lewis Lambert Strether. His careful modulation of the scenes and images that I have examined in the previous section seems to offer an adequate rebuttal of Garis's contention that the "last seven chapters turn against and annihilate the earlier ones." Only two years before, James had dealt with a flawed imagination in *The Sacred Fount*. There is no need to assume that this same theme suggested itself to him as a sudden "inspiration" after he had finished more than two-thirds of *The Ambassadors*. Strether bears a strange resemblance to the narrator of James's earlier novel. Like that frenzied builder of fantasies, "abused by a fine fancy," [17] Strether is victimized by his "free fancy" (p. 227). He, too, becomes intoxicated at the fountain of reality. He plays matchmaker with Miss Barrace and Waymarsh; he construes an affair between his friend and Sarah Pocock; he diverts Jim Pocock from his wife; he tries to pair off Mamie Pocock and little Bilham. Above all, he super-

---

[17] Henry James, *The Sacred Fount* (New York, Grove Press, 1953), p. 262. In the same passage Mrs. Brissenden goes on to accuse the crestfallen narrator of building up "houses of cards" based on imaginary relationships; in *The Ambassadors*, Strether complains smilingly that Mamie Pocock has "knocked down my tall house of cards" (p. 344).

imposes his own wishful distortions on the actual relationship between Mme. de Vionnet and Chad. His voracious imagination pulls him away from Maria Gostrey, whose unvarnished sense of reality is so unlike his own; it attracts him to Marie de Vionnet, whose deviousness gives him the illusion of pulling the oars of her barge. Strether quickly deprecates his relation with the all-knowing Miss Gostrey: "the time seemed already far off when he had held out his small thirsty cup to the spout of her pail. Her pail was scarce touched now, and *other fountains had flowed for him*" (p. 253, my italics).[18] Strether feasts himself on the lives of others but, in return, gives "nothing at all" (p. 203). His increasingly feverish excitement, his high-pitched professions to "see," and, of course, his ultimate defeat at the hands of reality, mark him as a distant but distinct cousin of the narrator of *The Sacred Fount*.

It is precisely the incongruity of Strether's dual kinship, his resemblance both to the ludicrous narrator as well as to Shakespeare's tragic hero, which converts him into a figure neither of comedy nor of tragedy, but a neutral figure of pathos. The narrator of *The Sacred Fount* tries to weld together the pieces of reality that he is allowed to observe through a keyhole; his failure is grotesquely comical. Antony, on the other hand, tries to weld the realities offered by two disintegrating cultures: he succeeds only through Cleopatra's death; his failure is a tragic triumph. Strether, though partaking of the modes of comedy and tragedy, is neither voyeur nor hero.[19] He delights in building imaginary relationships like those constructed by the ridiculous narrator, yet, at the same time, he has a sense of mission: he has come to France to create a higher law based on the polarities of Europe and America. His failure is pathetic. For Strether is mocked by the fragments he has been unable to weld. He drowns in the ocean that severs his cultural heritage because he can not bring himself to accept an actuality composed of extremes. The voyeurism of the narrator vitiates the nobility of Antony; the strict codes of Sarah Pocock nullify, and are nullified by, the refined deviousness of a Mme. de Vionnet. Only Maria Gostrey can bridge these extremes. The international lady who

---

[18] In *The American Henry James*, Anderson links Strether to the narrator of *The Sacred Fount* and alludes to the three images of the "fountain of life," the "sensuous sea in which we may drown," and the stream which cannot control the fountain, all of which James derived from his father's symbology (pp. 217ff.). James's intricate use of water-imagery in *The Ambassadors* certainly deserves a closer scrutiny than that accorded in my discussion of its connections to the Antony-Strether parallels.

[19] This distinction is not made by Fiedler, for whom Strether represents an impotent James's self-exaltation into the "Peeping Tom" as "hero" and "moral guide" (p. 337).

professes to be his "till death" (p. 56) is a real-life Cleopatra rejected by Strether. She alone is able to combine opposites at the cost of a moral ambiguity which Strether refuses to face: the ambiguity of life itself. Thus, the aged American must shrink from Maria as he has shrunk from Marie de Vionnet. He must be "sighed" away by her, "all comically, all tragically," and be written off as a pathetic failure (p. 465).[20]

In *Antony and Cleopatra*, Shakespeare's oblique allusions to Christianity indicate that the fragmented Pagan world left behind by Antony will be regenerated and bonded together by a new creed. The figure of Strether, on the other hand, stands between nineteenth-century doubt and twentieth-century alienation. Defeated by his romantic imagination, Strether has become inert. He has ceased to wander "between two worlds, one dead, / The other powerless to be born." But his inertia at least spares him from the more troublesome sight of Yeats's "rough beast," bent on renewing the worlds that he has lost through an apocalyptic blood-tide of anarchy.

---

[20] It is noteworthy that Strether's tragicomic leavetaking from Maria in chapter xxxvi is preceded by the pseudotragic farewell at Mme. de Vionnet's in chapter xxxiii and by the stridently "jocose" meeting with Chad in chapter xxxv.

Chronology of Important Dates

1843	Henry James, Jr., born April 15, in New York City, second son of Henry James and Mary Walsh.	
1843–44	First trip abroad to England and Paris.	Dickens, *Martin Chuzzlewit;* Emerson, *Essays, Second Series.*
1844–55	Childhood in Albany and New York.	
1855–59	Schooling and residence abroad —Paris, Boulogne, Geneva, Bonn. American home in Newport.	Flaubert, *Madame Bovary;* Darwin, *Origin of Species.*
1860–61	School and art study in Newport. "Obscure hurt" to James's back incurred fighting a fire.	Attack on Fort Sumter.
1862–63	Attended Harvard Law School	Battles of *Monitor* and *Merrimac,* Peninsula Campaign, Shiloh.
1865	"The Story of a Year," published in the *Atlantic Monthly.* Friendship with W. D. Howells.	End of Civil War; death of Lincoln; Whitman, *Drum-Taps.*
1870	Death of Minny Temple—the end of James's youth.	
1871	*Watch and Ward* ran as serial in *Atlantic Monthly*—James's first novel.	George Eliot, *Middlemarch.*
1876	Visit to Paris; settles in London; publishes *The American.*	French Impressionists; telephone invented; *The Adventures of Tom Sawyer.*

1878	*Daisy Miller* brings wide popularity; writes *The Europeans.*	Edison invents the electric light; Hardy, *The Return of the Native.*
1881	*The Portrait of a Lady.*	Ibsen, *Ghosts.*
1885	*The Bostonians* runs in the *Century Magazine* with *The Rise of Silas Lapham* and *Adventures of Huckleberry Finn.*	Zola, *Germinal;* Matthew Arnold, *Discourses in America.*
1890–95	*The Tragic Muse.* James's career as playwright culminates January 5, 1895, when he is booed from the stage at the premiere of *Guy Domville.* First notebook entry for *The Ambassadors.*	Ibsen; Wilde; William James, *Principles of Psychology;* Inernational Copyright; Wireless telegraph.
1897	*What Maisie Knew.* Settles at Lamb House, Rye.	Queen Victoria's Diamond Jubilee; Kipling.
1899–1900	*The Awkward Age. The Sacred Fount.*	Boer War; Freud, *Interpretation of Dreams;* Conrad, *Lord Jim.*
1902–04	Publication of *The Wings of the Dove, The Ambassadors,* and *The Golden Bowl.*	Wright brothers; Shaw; Chekhov, *The Cherry Orchard.*
1906–10	Visit to the United States and publication of *The American Scene.* New York Edition of selected works prepared and published.	Bergson, *Creative Evolution; Education of Henry Adams* written; Strindberg.
1913	*A Small Boy and Others. Notes of a Son and Brother.*	Proust; Stravinsky; D. H. Lawrence, *Sons and Lovers;* Frost, *A Boy's Will;* Sinking of the *Lusitania;* Einstein, *General Theory of Relativity.*
1915	James becomes British subject after outbreak of World War.	
1916	Death in Chelsea February 28. Ashes buried in Mount Auburn Cemetery, Cambridge, Mass.	

Notes on the Editor and Contributors

ALBERT E. STONE, JR., Professor of English at Emory University, is the author of *The Innocent Eye: Childhood in Mark Twain's Imagination* and the editor of books by Crèvecoeur and Mark Twain.

JOSEPH WARREN BEACH was for many years Professor of English at the University of Minnesota. Besides *The Method of Henry James,* his other important books were *The Concept of Nature in XIX-Century English Poetry* and *American Fiction: 1920–1940.*

ARNOLD BENNETT, a friend of James's as a young writer and drama critic, later wrote such novels as *The Old Wives' Tale, Clayhanger,* and *Riceyman Steps.*

JOAN BENNETT, Fellow of Girton College, Cambridge, is the author of *Five Metaphysical Poets* and studies of Virginia Woolf, George Eliot, and Sir Thomas Browne.

RICHARD P. BLACKMUR was a poet and Professor of English at Princeton University. He was the author of *Language as Gesture, The Double Agent,* and edited *The Art of the Novel,* James's collected Prefaces.

WAYNE C. BOOTH, Dean of the College, University of Chicago, published *The Rhetoric of Fiction* in 1961.

EDWARD KILLORAN BROWN was editor of the *University of Toronto Quarterly* and author of books on Matthew Arnold, Willa Cather, and Canadian poetry.

FREDERICK W. DUPEE is Professor of English at Columbia University and editor of *The Question of Henry James.*

LEON EDEL, Henry James Professor of English and American Letters at New York University, won the Pulitzer Prize in 1963 for his three-volume biography of James. He has written and edited many other books on James.

MAXWELL D. GEISMAR is a free-lance writer and a senior editor of *Ramparts* magazine. His books include *Rebels and Ancestors, Writers in Crisis,* and *American Moderns.*

ULRICH C. KNOEPFLMACHER, Associate Professor of English at the University of California, Berkeley, is the author of *Religious Humanism and the Victorian Novel: George Eliot, Walter Pater, and Samuel Butler.*

FRANK RAYMOND LEAVIS, Honorary Fellow of Downing College, Cambridge, founder of *Scrutiny*, is the author of such books as *New Bearings in English Poetry*, *Revaluation: Tradition and Development in English Poetry*, and *The Great Tradition: George Eliot, Henry James, Joseph Conrad.*

ANNIE R. M. LOGAN was a reviewer of books for *The Nation* and other magazines.

FRANCIS OTTO MATTHIESSEN, Professor of English at Harvard University, wrote *American Renaissance*, *The Achievement of T. S. Eliot*, and edited *The James Family*, and *The Notebooks of Henry James.*

ELIZABETH STEVENSON is the author of books on Henry Adams, Lafcadio Hearn, and the American 1920's, as well as *The Crooked Corridor: A Study of Henry James.*

JOHN E. TILFORD, JR., is Dean of the College of Arts and Sciences at Jacksonville University.

IAN WATT, author of *The Rise of the Novel*, is presently Professor of English at Stanford University.

YVOR WINTERS was a poet and Professor of English at Stanford University. Among his more influential critical works are *Primitivism and Decadence*, *Maule's Curse*, and *Anatomy of Nonsense.*

Selected Bibliography

The standard edition of *The Ambassadors* is the New York Edition of *The Novels and Tales of Henry James,* Volumes XXI and XXII (New York, 1909, reissued 1964). A corrected and annotated paperback text is the Norton Critical Edition (New York, W. W. Norton & Company, Inc., 1964), ed. S. P. Rosenbaum.

Leon Edel and Dan H. Laurence, *A Bibliography of Henry James,* 2nd ed., rev. (London, 1957, 1961) is the standard bibliography.

When completed, the definitive biography of Henry James will be that by Leon Edel, of which four volumes have been published: *Henry James: The Untried Years, 1843–1870; The Conquest of London, 1870–1881; The Middle Years, 1881–1895;* and *Henry James: The Treacherous Years, 1895–1901* (Philadelphia, 1953, 1962, 1969). An excellent one-volume critical biography is F. W. Dupee, *Henry James: His Life and Writings* (New York, 1951).

Among the many critical discussions of *The Ambassadors* the following are particularly valuable: Quentin Anderson, *The American Henry James* (New Brunswick, 1957); Oscar Cargill, *The Novels of Henry James* (New York, 1961); Richard Chase, "James's *Ambassadors"* in *Twelve Original Essays on Great American Novels,* ed. Charles Shapiro (Detroit, 1958), pp. 124–47; Frederick C. Crews, *The Tragedy of Manners: Moral Drama in the Later Novels of Henry James* (New Haven, 1957); Robert E. Garis, "The Two Lambert Strethers: A New Reading of *The Ambassadors,"* *Modern Fiction Studies,* VII (Winter, 1961–1962), 305–16; Barbara Hardy, *The Appropriate Form: An Essay on the Novel* (London, 1964); Lawrence B. Holland, *The Expense of Vision: Essays on the Craft of Henry James* (Princeton, 1964); David Lodge, *Language in Fiction: Essays in Criticism and Verbal Analysis of the English Novel* (London, 1966); Daniel J. Schneider, "The Ironic Imagery and Symbolism of James's *The Ambassadors,"* *Criticism,* IX (Spring, 1967), 174–96; Sister M. Corona Sharp, osu, *The Confidante in Henry James: Evolution and Moral Value of a Fictive Character* (Notre Dame, 1963); Robert W. Stallman, " 'The Sacred Rage': The Time-Theme in *The Ambassadors,"* *Modern Fiction Studies,* III (Spring, 1957), 41–56; J. A. Ward, *The Imagination of Disaster: Evil in the Fiction of Henry James* (Lincoln, 1961); Christof Wegelin, *The Image of Europe in Henry James* (Dallas, 1958); Orlo Williams, "*The Ambassadors,"* *Criterion,* VIII (September, 1928), 47–64.

TWENTIETH CENTURY
INTERPRETATIONS

MAYNARD MACK, *Series Editor*
Yale University

NOW AVAILABLE
Collections of Critical Essays
ON

ADVENTURES OF HUCKLEBERRY FINN
ALL FOR LOVE
THE AMBASSADORS
ARROWSMITH
AS YOU LIKE IT
BLEAK HOUSE
THE BOOK OF JOB
THE CASTLE
DOCTOR FAUSTUS
DUBLINERS
THE DUCHESS OF MALFI
EURIPEDES' ALCESTIS
THE FROGS
GRAY'S ELEGY
THE GREAT GATSBY
GULLIVER'S TRAVELS
HAMLET
HARD TIMES
HENRY IV, PART TWO
HENRY V
THE ICEMAN COMETH
JULIUS CAESAR
KEATS'S ODES

(continued on next page)

(continued from previous page)

LORD JIM
MUCH ADO ABOUT NOTHING
OEDIPUS REX
THE OLD MAN AND THE SEA
PAMELA
THE PLAYBOY OF THE WESTERN WORLD
THE PORTRAIT OF A LADY
A PORTRAIT OF THE ARTIST AS A YOUNG MAN
THE RIME OF THE ANCIENT MARINER
ROBINSON CRUSOE
SAMSON AGONISTES
THE SCARLET LETTER
SIR GAWAIN AND THE GREEN KNIGHT
THE SOUND AND THE FURY
THE TEMPEST
TOM JONES
TWELFTH NIGHT
UTOPIA
WALDEN
THE WASTE LAND
WUTHERING HEIGHTS